Strategic Community Partnerships,
Philanthropy, and Nongovernmental
Organization

T0327431

# Strategic Community Partnerships, Philanthropy, and Nongovernmental Organization

David J. Maurrasse

*Founder and President, Marga Incorporated; Adjunct Research Scholar, Earth Institute, and Associate Professor, School of International and Public Affairs, Columbia University, USA*

Cheltenham, UK • Northampton, MA, USA

Cover image: Pawel Czerwinski on Unsplash.

Published by
Edward Elgar Publishing Limited
The Lypiatts
15 Lansdown Road
Cheltenham
Glos GL50 2JA
UK

Edward Elgar Publishing, Inc.
William Pratt House
9 Dewey Court
Northampton
Massachusetts 01060
USA

Paperback edition 2023

A catalogue record for this book
is available from the British Library

Library of Congress Control Number: 2021945178

This book is available electronically in the **Elgar**online
Political Science and Public Policy subject collection
http://dx.doi.org/10.4337/9781788979085

ISBN 978 1 78897 907 8 (cased)
ISBN 978 1 78897 908 5 (eBook)
ISBN 978 1 0353 1212 2 (paperback)

Printed and bound by CPI Group (UK) Ltd, Croydon, CR0 4YY

# Contents

# Acknowledgements

As usual, a book project is a communal endeavor. In some ways, it is like the partnerships profiled in this book. It requires funding and collaboration across numerous individuals and institutions. So, this text is a product of the efforts of so many to whom I am grateful.

I would like to begin by thanking the New World Foundation, and Colin Greer, its president, in particular. I have worked with Colin and New World in various capacities for over two decades. This connection has produced various ideas and initiatives intended to strengthen communities and expand opportunities for underserved populations. The New World Foundation's ongoing support for my research allows for continuous exploration of innovative ways in which resources are leveraged, through philanthropy and partnerships, to solve pressing social issues. As a true veteran in philanthropy, Colin maintains an exuberantly exploratory mind. His steadfast support for scholarly inquiry as a pathway to understanding strategies for community-based solutions is so greatly appreciated. I am so fortunate to be a beneficiary of this thinking.

I consider myself a hybrid between a scholar and a practitioner. My business, Marga Incorporated, has been my practice for many years. Alongside my practice has been Columbia University. I would like to thank Columbia University's Earth Institute for being a home for my research over recent years. Through this base, I have been able to hire numerous interns. The person who handles numerous logistics including managing my interns, Hayley Martinez, deserves special acknowledgement.

Research for this book spanned a few semesters, including a few under a pandemic. Some interns worked on this project over multiple terms, and some worked for a single term. Therefore, it was always an art to pass responsibilities from one group of interns to another. I would like to express my sincere thanks to the following interns: Chaarvi Amit Badani, Victoria Bortfeld, Haley Campbell, Michele Favero, Maria Harker, Carolina de Los Angeles Sakshi Mishra, Sam Sheldon, Christopher Taktak, Leiva Ureta, and Jason West. I would like to highlight the important role played by Haley Campbell in the first section of this book, Jason West and Christopher Taktak regarding United States-based community partnerships, and Maria Harker and Sam Sheldon regarding international community partnerships. Victoria Bortfeld deserves special thanks for working on all aspects of the book and helping me to tie everything together. I would also like to thank Shangchao

Liu from Marga Incorporated for helping to design the book project from the beginning and refine it to the very end.

Thanks to Edward Elgar Publishing for publishing this book. My first book with Edward Elgar focused on public–private partnerships. This book essentially builds on the other book, but with an explicit intent to highlight the nonprofit sector and philanthropy. I expressed to Edward Elgar that I wanted to underscore that the multistakeholder partnerships that are having the greatest impact at the community level are driven by nonprofit organizations with the support of private philanthropy. They gave me the opportunity to expand on the idea of community partnerships, which are often more dynamic and comprehensive than many collaborative efforts that are limited to government and private industry. Community partnerships rely on the "third sector," beyond the public and private sectors.

Finally, I would like to appreciate the important work of all 10 of the community partnerships from across the United States and around the world which are profiled in this book. These initiatives provide important insights on how individuals and organizations in communities can creatively harness local assets to improve lives and solve pressing social and economic problems. Particularly given the widespread impacts of the COVID-19 pandemic, which has devastated communities around the world, we will be in greater need of strategic thinking and action to improve health, to expand economic and educational opportunity, and to address numerous other concerns.

# 1. Introduction

Turbulent times are upon us. Tens of millions of people have contracted COVID-19. Hundreds of thousands have died from it. An economic crisis has accompanied this public health emergency – a global pandemic. Entire industries have been rattled, disrupted, or even tragically devastated by necessary shutdowns. Millions have lost jobs. Job loss has a domino effect, as people can no longer cover their basic costs, especially housing. Government intervention has prevented people from experiencing evictions or foreclosures. But government will provide this support for only so long. Dramatic increases in homelessness are underway and inevitable. As vaccinations continue, seeking to slow the spread of the pandemic, there is some hope for a better future. However, the long-term impacts of the pandemic will be felt for years to come.

The health consequences of the pandemic and the economic adversity that has impacted so many have certainly been presenting new challenges. However, it is increasingly the case that they have largely exacerbated existing ones. The *social determinants of health* tell us that health outcomes are the result of the neighborhoods in which we live, the air we breathe, the jobs we hold, and so many other nonclinical factors. Therefore, lower-income people have greater health challenges, as do populations that have historically experienced discrimination due to race or other factors. In the United States, it has been very apparent that people of color (especially Black, Latinx, and Native populations) have contracted COVID-19 more frequently and died from the virus at higher rates. Economically, these same groups have been experiencing higher rates of unemployment and are disproportionately concentrated in low-wage jobs that cannot be conducted remotely. They are also living in closer quarters, in many cases in multigenerational households. Consequently, the pandemic highlighted existing longstanding inequities. The difficulties experienced by communities of color and lower-income populations during the pandemic demonstrated ongoing vulnerabilities.

Another existing inequity highlighted during the pandemic was police brutality and racist violence. The Black Lives Matter movement has drawn tens of millions of all races into levels of sustained protest not seen since the Civil Rights Movement. Protesters have not only called for police and criminal justice reform; they have forced a global dialogue on systemic racism. The kinds of historical health and economic disparities laid perilously bare during the COVID-19 pandemic exemplify manifestations of systemic racism. In all facets of life, inequities influenced by race over generations are being noticeably challenged. One other area in which racial disparities have been apparent during the pandemic is education. As school instruction became remote and virtual, those without computers or internet at home and without adequate working space at home fell further behind.

Between the exhibition of the price of persistent systemic racism during the pandemic and the growth of a racial justice movement catalyzed by outrage over racially biased police brutality, COVID-19 and Black Lives Matter are linked. The pandemic deepened systemic racism, and the contemporary racial justice movement forged and revived a call to action to end it. In the midst of the many complex and daunting circumstances of the year 2020, many have been working together to respond. When considering a tragedy as sweeping as a global pandemic, it is clear that various actors are required to collaborate and coordinate to bring about solutions. Government must take clear and decisive action at all levels, from the nation to the localized district. But so many others must play a role. Hospitals must care for patients. They need adequate capacity to do so, and keep their own staff safe in the process. When hospitals did not have capacity, places such as parks, convention centers, and stadiums were used for additional beds. Corporations repurposed production to create needed medical supplies. Foundations created funds to help communities devastated by the crisis. Medical schools graduated students early so they could more quickly practice medicine and fight the virus. University research has been helping public understanding of the virus and contributing to finding a vaccine. University dorms have been used for various purposes. Community-based nonprofit organizations of various types have been working with local communities and helping them deal with limited income and food insecurity. Numerous types of institutions have been helping with testing and contact tracing. Many institutions have also intervened to help bridge the digital divide, as so many have been thrust into relying on virtual forms of learning and work.

Overall, the pandemic, its public health and economic consequences, and the aim to dismantle systemic racism require the participation of numerous sectors and types of organizations. But societies are not naturally organized into series of cross-sector partnerships that can be deployed whenever necessary. Rather, society tends to be organized more separately in professional and industrial silos. Crises tend to test these boundaries and force communication about common interests and the need to coordinate resources and expertise across government, civil society, and the private and nonprofit sectors. This is particularly true in neighborhoods, cities or towns, and regions. Localities are comprised of ecosystems of organizations and institutions representing a variety of fields and sectors. These organizations and institutions have their own singular missions, but they exist in interdependent settings. This interdependence is not always openly acknowledged or appreciated, but in times of crisis, it becomes much more apparent.

Geographical location is also significant in the lived experiences of those who reside in a given area. The effects of the pandemic and its broader repercussions are felt and experienced in places. Indeed, the pandemic crystallized this reality, as it focused on homes. It called for many to "shelter in place." In the process, those residing in larger homes could socially distance. Those with careers conducive to working at home could stay employed and maintain their income. Those who contracted the virus and needed medical attention would go to the closest hospital. They also needed health insurance to do so. Hospitals serving wealthier communities have more substantial resources than those serving lower-income and underinsured populations. On so many levels, our daily realities during the pandemic reminded us of the significance of place.

The collection of different types of organizations in localities and regions varies from place to place. Certainly, every community has its unique qualities. For example, some areas are not even close to a hospital. But if people must drive an hour to a hospital in a neighboring community, this population of patients is in the hospital's orbit. These are circumstances we are more likely to see in rural areas. Each local ecosystem of institutions is different. There is no single geographical distance to define the boundaries of these ecosystems. They simply vary from one community to the next. In some densely populated areas, the conception of "community" might be a neighborhood. But, usually, a community-based ecosystem extends beyond single neighborhoods.

The idea for this book was conceived long before the advent of COVID-19. But the dynamics of the pandemic and the myriad illustrations of inequities around it only reinforced the importance of *community partnerships*. Coordinated efforts among different institutions and organizations sharing in common a geographic locality intended to strengthen their surroundings by both expanding opportunities for their geographical place and reducing inequities and injustices facing their populations are going to be fundamental to rebuilding and reimagining in the wake of COVID-19. Many residents in various neighborhoods, cities, and regions will be in dire need of attention to their health, employment opportunities, quality education, sufficient housing, food, and more. Especially with so many lives further disrupted by the pandemic, government can do only so much. We have seen government intervention to keep people employed and to provide income during COVID-19 shutdowns. These actions underscored the importance of government. But these are temporary benefits. In the absence of these benefits, especially given the extent of job losses, some communities will buckle under the pressure. The lost income and wealth, long-term health and education consequences, and other factors will impact communities for years to come, not to mention the restructuring of how we live our lives given the ease of spreading a virus such as COVID-19. Communities will have to be organized, and the institutions in local ecosystems will have to be leveraged and coordinated. Community partnerships, such as those profiled herein, have reached a defining moment, as they will be called upon like never before.

Before the emergence of COVID-19, persistent inequities in health and education were among many characteristics confronting an ever more complex world. We are more interconnected than ever before, but the effects of climate change, hunger, or homelessness are demonstrated at the community level, urban or rural, in developing or developed nations. The United Nations' Sustainable Development Goals (SDGs)[1] have been an international approach to simultaneously address today's multifaceted array of social and economic challenges. While their intentions are global, the implementation of the SDGs strategies are ultimately local, involving agreements with national governments and various partners down to the level of neighborhoods.

At the community level, we find an ecosystem of people and institutions. From one neighborhood, city, or region to the next, the nature of these population demographics and institutional actors vary. These people and organizations exist in interdependent spaces. Their destinies are aligned in some way, even in the midst of vast inequities. For example, when a city has a declining tax base, social services diminish, affecting schools, roads, public transportation, public health, and numerous other factors. This reality is happening right now, as the COVID-19 pandemic dramatically reduced tax revenues at various levels of government, leading to significant cuts.[2] Indeed, the actual impact of these circumstances most adversely shapes the lives of the most vulnerable segments of populations. These are the people whose lives are most influenced by such systems and services. But these dynamics also impact institutions large and small. A business depending on a local customer base, a hospital, a university, arts institutions, and others, are all directly impacted by a declining local economy.

This book focuses on particular aspects of the development and implementation of multistakeholder collaborative initiatives – *community partnerships* – based in and focused on neighborhoods, municipalities, and regions. These community partnerships can include representation from numerous different types of organizations across the public, private, and nongovernmental spectrum. In observing these collaborative efforts, two dynamics are particularly emphasized in this book – the role of private philanthropic institutions and their resources in facilitating the creation and continuation of these partnerships, along with the role of nongovernmental organizations of various types (from grassroots community-based organizations to universities and hospitals) as important enduring institutions in localities that have historically not been fully tapped as agents of community and economic development.

The intentions of these partnerships are important distinguishing factors. These community partnerships are focused on a common good that transcends the interests of a particular organization, sector, or field. For example, a chamber of commerce may bring together businesses across various fields in a geographical area, but for the purpose of advocating for the interests of the business community. Certainly, chambers of commerce vary in their priorities, and some ultimately seek broader improvements beyond business interests. A community partnership, however, would convene with the primary intent of strengthening a locality. Partnerships come in many different forms. Certainly, various studies have sought to enhance understanding of partnerships on numerous levels. This book's contribution to the base of existing literature is further highlighting an exploration of collaborative initiatives that are locally based and locally focused with significant participation of the nonprofit sector and philanthropy.

These efforts are important because they are increasingly crucial in how society solves problems. The involvement of the nongovernmental sector and philanthropy in these efforts is worthy of particular exploration, because these entities have social missions that can be more naturally extended to the pursuit of a more common good in a locality or region. We have seen this demonstrated in the role of hospitals during the COVID-19 pandemic. These institutions are already committed to addressing health needs. This purpose is extended to helping communities serve the public amidst a public health crisis. Government, nonprofits, and philanthropy can work together with hospitals on various levels – public awareness, the production and distribution of personal protective equipment, and the use of additional locations to provide testing and vaccination.

While the concept of public/private partnerships, focused on cooperation between government and business, has gotten significant attention, the role of nonprofit organizations and philanthropy in collaborative efforts across sectors and involving multiple stakeholders deserves further exploration. Philanthropic funding can provide partnerships the flexible capital required in order to convene, assess, reflect, and strategize. Donors can attract attention and bring people and institutions together that would not ordinarily come to the table. Grassroots nonprofits can provide representative voices of local residents in partnerships. Larger nonprofits such as universities bring a unique blend of resources that enhance partnerships. These realities are particularly pronounced in locally based and focused collaborations – representing the significance of community partnerships.

## NOTES

1. The 17 SDGs, presented in the UN 2030 Agenda for Sustainable Development, are an urgent call for action by all countries – developed and developing – in a global partnership. They recognize that ending poverty and other deprivations must go hand in hand with strategies that improve health and education, reduce inequality, and spur economic growth – all while tackling climate change and working to preserve our oceans and forests.
2. From March through May 2020, 34 states experienced at least a 20% drop in revenue compared with the same period last year, according to data provided to National Public Radio by the State and Local Finance Initiative. With dwindling cash, cuts to education, health care, and other areas are inevitable in many places. For example, Maryland has cut *nearly $190 million from higher education* as of August 2020.

# PART I

# Philanthropy, nongovernmental organizations, and community partnership

# 2.   Evolving thinking on community partnerships

The notion of collaborative efforts involving multiple stakeholders working toward some common good has received increasing attention among scholars and practitioners. Recent literature has addressed the purpose, design, and formation of partnerships. Partnerships form to address myriad societal problems at different scales, ranging from global partnerships to facilitate progress on development goals (Maurrasse, 2018; MacDonald et al., 2018) to partnerships at the municipal level as exemplified in the ENRICH Study (Spencer-Hwang et al., 2016).

While partnerships are increasingly cross-sectoral, *managing* the business sector continues to receive special attention in the literature on strategy and the common good (Bendell, 2011). This is perhaps a consequence of the competition between public good logic and market logic that plays out within cross-sectoral partnerships (Ashraf et al., 2017). Literature on multistakeholder, place-based work tends to center the public interest more often than literature on other forms of strategic partnership (see Cantor et al., 2019; Pribbenow and Beeth, 2019). A growing number of cross-sectoral partnerships are organizing around theories of change (van Tulder and Keen, 2018). Further investigation is required to determine whether this trend will lead to greater emphasis on the common good in partnerships at the various levels.

The performance of partnerships has also been an emphasis in recent literature. Successful partnerships are designed and implemented with a clear objective. Strategic pursuit of a common good depends on partners' ability to track progress toward their objective. Assessing the performance of these kinds of partnerships involves collecting data that provide some measure of the public good – for a health systems partnership such data might include number of hospital visits per capita, for example. Van Tulder et al. (2016) advanced a framework for discussing impact assessment with regard to cross-sectoral partnerships. Impact appears to be one of the most fertile grounds for research on strategy, partnership, and the common good moving forward. Clarke and MacDonald (2016) have taken another approach to impact in partnerships – a resource-based view on outcomes to participants in multistakeholder, cross-sectoral partnerships. Writing on monitoring and evaluation, two important elements of strategic thinking, will explore new frontiers as demand rises for disaggregated data in the community development field. While a similar trend is possible in strategic partnership at larger scales, it is not yet suggested by the literature.

Our understanding of partnerships could be further enhanced with some emphasis on geographic place. Community partnerships focusing on improving conditions in a locality occupy an important space in this landscape, because they tend to be solution oriented. They are also poised to have some demonstrable impact due to a more manageable scale than a national or global partnership. The community partnerships featured herein are solutions oriented. They tend to focus on some version of a common good within their locality or region. But these foci are manifested in a wide variety of ways.

These partnerships are *strategic* because they are faced with a range of options, and must assess their assets and circumstances in order to determine their path.[1] Some of the featured partnerships in this book were designed for a single purpose, and intend to dissolve upon completing their goals. Others are designed to remain in place for some time so that they can not only address a set of problems in the short term, but so they can be available to handle the challenges of the future. Community partnerships can bring longstanding value, as they constitute new forms of governance that enable ongoing communication and coordination across a group of actors sharing a neighborhood, city, or region. Strategically, the endurance of such partnerships can bring important value as new challenges arise, particularly in times of crisis. This dynamic has become evident given the extraordinary circumstances of 2020.

## THE CURRENT CONTEXT AND PARTNERSHIPS

The current context of a global pandemic and its aftermath alongside a widespread racial reckoning catalyzed by the Black Lives Matter movement have highlighted vast longstanding inequities. In the COVID-19 pandemic, lower-income populations and communities of color have been facing disproportionate adverse impacts.[2] These daunting realities, from high death rates to significant unemployment to vulnerability in housing and a lack of resources for young people to participate in remote learning, are all manifested in places – in the neighborhoods and cities or towns in which people reside. The pandemic has demonstrated the precariousness of the livelihoods of substantial percentages of populations in the United States (U.S.) and elsewhere. Persistent inequities among large segments of society lead to instability. For example, in areas in which COVID-19 cases rise, hospitals become overrun. They may not have the space to handle the influx of new patients with COVID-19 or any other health condition. As the coronavirus presents particular challenges to those with pre-existing conditions, populations that have traditionally lacked access to health care or healthy food or clean air or adequate housing will be the ones overwhelmingly in those hospital beds. In recent years, there has been increasing awareness about *social determinants of health*, demonstrating that health outcomes are largely influenced by nonclinical, societal factors (i.e. income, zip code, etc.).[3] In the pandemic, many lower-income workers were considered "essential" – employed in supermarkets, drug stores, and public transportation. These workers could not work remotely like many others. They were out of their homes and among patrons. At earlier stages in the pandemic, these essential workers were even more vulnerable, as experts were still learning more about how the virus spreads and how people can protect themselves and others. Many of these essential workers contracted the virus and died. At home, many lower-income workers may not have much space to enable social distancing. They may live in multigenerational households with little square footage. Therefore, one worker who contracts the virus could bring it home to relatives.

This is one example of the dynamics of inequality. When considering the breadth of issues confronting lower-income communities, it is hard to imagine the depth of investment and collaboration necessary to even begin to turn these situations around. As societies shut down during the pandemic, national governments had to figure out how to keep society afloat. In various parts of the world, stimulus packages were required, providing income and unemployment benefits. In the U.S., the over $2 trillion in stimulus from the CARES Act proved miniscule.[4] With each government intervention comes a protracted and highly politicized tug of war. Indeed, we need more effective government. The pandemic has also exhibited the value of what some call "big government." Government is responsible for populations, and should do as much as possible to provide a safety net and support basic necessities. However, the pressing issues facing local communities, laid bare during the pandemic, increasingly require the inclusion of private philanthropic resources and nongovernmental organizations to complement the capabilities of government and public agencies to meet societal needs, reduce inequities, and expand opportunities for vulnerable populations.

This was evident during the pandemic, as philanthropic and collaborative initiatives intervened to provide financial assistance, food, health services, personal protective equipment (PPE), facilities, and a variety of other needs. For example, a partnership between the Astros Foundation and Crane Worldwide Logistics was announced in April 2020. The partnership's objective was to not only deliver essential PPE to Houston hospitals within the Texas Medical Center, but to provide support through funding, transportation services, and distribute other necessary medical supplies used by health-care professionals. Since the partnership's conception, approximately 10.7 million masks, 400,000 nasal swabs, 200,000 face shields and 30,000 googles have been delivered along with an additional $400,000 donation provided by the Astros

Foundation. Crane Worldwide Logistics was able to utilize its connections and collect PPE from around the globe, and the Astros Foundation leveraged relationships within the City of Houston to contribute an enormous amount of critical supplies.

Furthermore, as the initial epicentre in the U.S., activity in the New York City area was significantly interrupted by the COVID-19 pandemic. A dramatic increase in demand for grocery delivery services and food provision followed the shutdown, particularly for immunocompromised and vulnerable city residents who could not safely venture outside. Nonprofit organizations such as RiseBoro Community Partnership, in collaboration with organizations like Grow NYC and World Central Kitchen (WCK), have bolstered efforts to provide healthy foods to help feed hospitalized populations, at-risk individuals, and their families. Prior to the pandemic, RiseBoro typically provided services for 160 people per week. As national unemployment skyrocketed, the organization averaged at serving 1,200 vulnerable individuals per week, equating to 900 lbs of produce each week. This community partnership is successfully able to meet this growing demand through the contribution of safely, individually packaged fresh meals provided by Grow NYC and WCK, and the utilization of RiseBoro's community ties to effectively distribute these food parcels to struggling neighborhoods.

As individual entities, foundations, community-based organizations, universities, hospitals, corporations, and others can make vital contributions. But through collaboration, they can combine their resources toward greater ends. Today's complex challenges are best met with expertise and resources from across industries and sectors.[5] Additionally, the pandemic also reminded us of the importance of coordination. The public health and economic crises that emerged due to COVID-19 required a great deal of coordinated action. If there was a need for more hospital beds, where would one turn? Where could students without computers at home get access to laptops and the internet? How could PPE get to hospitals and to residents in a given locality? These were immediate needs during the height of an outbreak. But they reflect an ongoing reality – communities must band together if they are to be prepared for crises. Because deep inequities magnify the impact and devastation caused by a crisis, it is in a broader community's best interest to collaborate and work to reduce inequities. As so many have lost jobs,[6] for example, communities will be best served getting employers across sectors involved in providing the necessary networking, training, and placement to increase local employment. This will lead to a better functioning society. Many small businesses have not been able to make it through the pandemic. If communities want to keep the services these businesses provide to a community going, it is in their best interest to act collaboratively to rectify the situation. We certainly need more effective and robust government to intervene and make sure that small businesses don't close.[7] In the U.S., the CARES Act attempted to do this. It worked in some instances, and not in others. It was exploited by some who did not need the resources. But, overall, it simply was not enough.

This is where private philanthropy and nongovernmental organizations can play a crucial role. The potential of this role can be magnified through collaboration. This book highlights various case examples of collaborative initiatives involving numerous stakeholders representing different fields and industries that are specifically intended to address an issue or series of issues facing localities.

In a prior publication, *Strategic Public Private Partnerships* (Maurrasse, 2013), I noted that strategic partnerships were becoming important vehicles through which various institutions and stakeholders combine resources and expertise to jointly solve problems or produce innovations. The use of the terminology "public private partnerships" captures one important dimension of how these collaborative efforts are transforming how we consider the role of government, the concept of public service, and the tools applied to addressing many of society's most pressing challenges.

This book is placing a greater emphasis on community partnerships in particular, and the unique contributions of private philanthropy and various nonprofit organizations within them. Community partnerships are important because, as the pandemic tragically exhibited, the great obstacles that society must overcome are experienced by people in their localities. Ideally, communities would not have to be concerned about access to health care, paying rent or mortgages, getting quality public schooling, feeling safe, or any number of matters. In such a scenario, a combination of local and national governments would have adequate resources to meet these needs for everyone. In some parts of the world, this is closer to reality than in others. Especially in the U.S., but in other parts of the world, residents and institutions in localities are increasingly looking beyond government to leverage resources and expertise that can improve their surroundings. Local leaders are thinking broadly about which institutions should play a role in community and economic development. It is becoming very apparent that nongovernmental organizations, such as philanthropic institutions, locally focused nonprofit organizations, and enduring institutions such as universities and hospitals are playing a crucial role in catalyzing and sustaining multistakeholder, cross-sector partnerships. In discussions of public private partnerships, there has not been adequate attention paid to this highly significant dynamic. Private philanthropy is providing the flexible capital to enable and sustain many of these partnerships. As I maintained in *Strategic Public Private Partnerships* (Maurrasse, 2013), these formations become entities in themselves with their own structure, needs, and expenses. Also, as our technologically driven times have withered physical boundaries, geographical places still matter. Some of the most compelling cross-sector collaborative initiatives are taking root in places. Place-based community partnerships are leveraging resources, with the substantial leadership and participation of nongovernmental organizations, to increase access to opportunities for vulnerable populations, improve natural disaster preparedness, enhance health delivery, and strengthen local schooling.

A few books focus on the relationship between philanthropic organizations and community development via case study analysis. *Catalysts for Change: 21st Century Philanthropy and Community Development* by Martinez-Cosio and Bussell (2013) discusses the history of philanthropic funding and demonstrates five case studies across America. The authors maintain that no single model fits all situations, and highlight the importance of context and stakeholder relationships in community development initiatives. The book *Unequal Partnerships: Beyond the Rhetoric of Philanthropic Collaboration* by Silver (2005) is primarily based on the case study of Chicago Initiative, which is one of 50 nationwide U.S. initiatives dedicated to addressing poverty via collaboration and partnerships between foundations and community-based organizations. The author critically analyzed the case and found the initiative enabled community-based organizations to influence funding flows, which led to the undesired reproduction of the local elite's power. Despite the facts and findings of these books, they are relatively specific case-focused studies and do not comprehensively explore the rationale for foundations' role in partnerships in general.

Some books address the role of foundations in cross-sector partnerships generally. *Partnerships the Nonprofit Way: What Matters, What Doesn't* by Mendel and Brudney (2018) covers the successes and failures of 52 nonprofit leaders and summarizes the characteristics of nonprofit organizations as well as practices that make collaboration successful. Philanthropic cross-sector partnerships are also examined from private, corporate, or other perspectives by several books. The book *Unicorns Unite: How Nonprofits and Foundations Can Build EPIC Partnerships* by Shams-Lau et al. (2018) focuses on the relationship between nonprofits and foundations by examining the philosophies and practices that prevent the collaboration between foundations and other nonprofit organizations. *Doing Best by Doing Good: How to Use Public Purpose Partnerships to Boost Corporate Profits and Benefit your Community* by Steckel and Simons (1992) includes several corporate philanthropy examples such as IBM and American Express to guide the use of corporate philanthropy as a marketing tool. The book *Putting partnerships to work: Strategic Alliances for Development Between Government, the Private Sector and Civil Society* by Warner and Sullivan (2017) discusses partnerships by using practical examples in the oil, gas, and mining industries.

Some other books stress the role of philanthropy in global governance and development. These global development experiences could be valuable and insightful in understanding the role of foundations in community partnerships. The book *Private Foundations and Development Partnerships: American Philanthropy and Global Development Agendas* by Moran (2014) analyzed the influence of private U.S. philanthropic foundations in global governance and development issues via a close scrutiny of several case studies of public–private collaboration. In the chapter "Partnerships and urban governance" of the book *Partnerships in Urban Governance: European and American Experiences* by Pierre (1998), partnerships are briefly mentioned and examined from the perspective of urban governance; the rationale and benefits of public and private partnership are briefly discussed.

While there is relevant content in these books, the particular role of philanthropic institutions and larger enduring nonprofit organizations as agents of change in community-based partnerships requires further exploration.

## METHODS

The findings in this book are based on an examination of community partnerships throughout the world. A team of researchers at Columbia University's Earth Institute conducted extensive online research to identify examples of community partnerships to be further investigated. We were seeking a few characteristics of partnerships to profile. The partnerships identified have been in existence for two or more years, so that we could identify a track record. The intent of the research is to investigate the unique contributions of various types of nonprofit organizations as well as private philanthropy to community partnerships. These partnerships include various stakeholders, representing different sectors and industries. These partnerships are also in existence in order to mitigate or solve social and economic concerns in their geographic places.

Once partnerships were identified to be profiled, the research team investigated further, guided by a particular framework: background on the partnership; the partnership's strategy (if it has an explicit strategic plan or its purpose, goals, and intentions); the role of nonprofit/nongovernmental organizations in the partnership; the unique value of these organizations to the partnership; the partnership's impact; the factors that contributed to success; and the effort's future intentions. We deliberately selected partnerships that could articulate some impact or success. Ten partnerships were selected to be profiled – five in the U.S. and five in various parts of the world (intentionally spread across different continents). The profiles of these partnerships are essentially snapshots of their characteristics. There is much more that could have been captured on each of these community partnerships. The intent of the profiles is to highlight salient characteristics. Some of the profiles emphasize the partners in greater depth. In some other instances, the impact of the partnership is more compelling. Therefore, these particular profiles included greater elaboration on what the partnership has been able to achieve. Some of the partnerships have been in existence for longer periods, thus there might be more to say about their history and achievements.

The uniqueness of our times, with the COVID-19 pandemic, had to be addressed in some way. Therefore, some of the profiles include the various ways in which the partnership responded to the pandemic in its community. Not all of the partnerships had evidence of activity specifically geared toward the pandemic. But where we could find this information, we thought it would be important to include it. One reason for this is the manner in which the pandemic, as manifested in localities, illustrated the importance of collaboration and coordination. It is therefore not surprising that some of our profiled community partnerships had somewhat robust activities in the face of the virus and its public health, economic, and overall societal impacts.

A few of the profiled partnerships are in the U.S., where such formations are more plentiful than in other parts of the world. This is largely due to the significant breadth of philanthropy and the nonprofit sector in the U.S. But we also profiled partnerships beyond the U.S., and sought to represent Europe, Asia, Africa, and South America. Profiles were developed based on additional online exploration as well as direct outreach to the partnerships' leadership. Due to the pace of change in the current context, we periodically reached out to the partnerships and updated the profiles. We intentionally included, where possible, these partnerships' efforts to address the pandemic in their communities and any approaches to address manifestations of systemic racism in their localities. Once the profiles were completed, researchers highlighted relevant themes as well as evidence of the unique contributions of nonprofit organizations and private philanthropy to the impact of the partnerships. We reviewed common themes across the partnerships, which informed the analysis and conclusions in this book.

## COMMUNITY PARTNERSHIPS

Collaborative initiatives designed to strengthen local communities through directly addressing important social and economic concerns deserve particular attention. Partnerships come in many forms and pursue any number of imaginable goals. Community partnerships have a particular utility. In the midst of the many issues in our current context, even the ability to ensure fair elections, community partnerships can play a crucial role. Furthermore, the nongovernmental sector and private philanthropy are unique contributors to the capacity of community partnerships to solve problems. It is also likely that some of the issues confronting localities simply cannot be solved without community partnerships, which bring together and harness the resources and expertise of local institutions, government, and community residents.

Considering the breadth of work that will be required to rebuild and reimagine communities in the wake of the COVID-19 pandemic, it is difficult to envision significant progress without the coordination and collaboration of numerous local organizations. The pandemic led to dramatic unemployment, deepened educational inequities, long-term health consequences, and numerous disruptions. Government alone can handle only so much. This reality has been demonstrated throughout the pandemic. For instance, in order to support unmet public health and economic needs during the pandemic, philanthropic partnerships have taken root to create new funding for organizations that directly serve communities that are disproportionately impacted as a result of COVID-19. The Seattle Foundation was among the earliest to respond to the pandemic in its community. In March 2020, a coalition of Seattle-area philanthropy, government, and business partners launched the COVID-19 Response Fund which distributed grant funds to community-based recipients identified by the Seattle Foundation. The first round of grants distributed more than $10 million to 128 nonprofits navigating the immediate economic and health impacts of the pandemic. In mid-June, Phase 2 grants deployed $9.2 million to 220 nonprofits and coalitions, focusing on child care, mental and behavior health, and emergency financial assistance.

Following the actions of the Seattle Foundation, other philanthropic organizations took steps to distribute much needed financial assistance. For instance, the New York Community Trust in partnership with the Nonprofit Finance Fund administered the NYC COVID-19 Response and Impact Fund to aid essential nonprofit service providers. Only a month after its launch date, the fund raised more than $95 million, surpassing its initial goal of $75 million, from over 500 foundations, corporations, and individual donors. The award prioritized human service organizations that provided direct assistance in areas of health care, housing, and food insecurity.

Community partnerships must be strategic – they must make careful choices about their overall goals and objectives as well as the specific projects they wish to pursue. Some community partnerships are short term, existing in order to resolve a particular problem before dissolving. Others are longer term, and sometimes develop broader agendas for the overall well-being of a geographical area. Some community partnerships settle on a particular number of partners and do not intentionally grow, while others continue to add partners. Of course, so many variables influence the experiences of community partnerships – the size of the locality, the degree of challenges facing the community, the types of institutions situated in the community, and others.

Strategic choices among community partnerships are relevant at various stages in the development of a collaborative initiative, as well as in moments of crisis. In the *formative* stages, partnerships are confronted with how to come together, which institutions should be represented in the partnership, what should be the initial goals of the partnership, and how should it define success. In the *intermediate* stages of development, partnerships must consider how to maintain their work if they intend to continue, how to expand or contract, and how to maximize their impact. Partnerships at this stage in the life cycle are often re-examining their capacity and limitations. They are focusing their strategic points of emphasis. They are beyond their initial visioning of the formative stage. *Advanced* community partnerships are aware of the framework that they have established. They have developed an ongoing way to leverage the combined resources of institutions in their community. They enable coordination across a wide range of different types of institutions across sectors, all of which have their own unique missions. Their missions may not explicitly emphasize community and economic development, but the partnership becomes a hub through which various stakeholders can gather around a common interest. The institutions all share an inherent vested interest in improving their locality. They are challenged to be inclusive and to democratically engage broader populations. They are also challenged to ensure that their efforts are equitable, seeking to reduce rather than exacerbate longstanding inequities in their communities.

These various dynamics make community partnerships compelling. Very different types of partners, which may not naturally collaborate professionally, come together around a collective interest in local conditions. But local conditions are complex, and these partnerships must be aware and driven by values that ensure the most underserved segments of local populations benefit from their efforts. They essentially reside in an ecosystem in which they are bound together. This reality becomes particularly apparent in *crises*. The pandemic, for example, forces a common experience, but it also highlights inequities. Communities experiencing a significant COVID-19 outbreak face a lockdown and require action from wherever resources are available. Institutions with space must make it available. Institutions with access to medical supplies must do what they can to disseminate them appropriately. Institutions must transcend typical operating procedures to contribute to a broader cause. Community partnerships that are already in existence when a crisis arises are positioned to coordinate resources across institutions, and communicate with government.

At every stage of development of a community partnership, and in moments of crisis, nonprofit/nongovernmental organizations and private philanthropy are fundamental to developing and executing partnerships' strategies. Nonprofit/nongovernmental organizations of varying sizes bring a social mission, some of which include a mission centered on improving their local community. Private philanthropy brings financial resources, often flexible, that allow partnerships to advance their work. Community partnerships require time, and they create new expenses. Private philanthropic resources can bring financial capital to cover expenses as well as support the necessary time for reflection, analysis, and strategic dialogue. Additionally, some private foundations, such as community foundations, are explicitly focused on strengthening their localities. Therefore, community partnerships essentially serve as an extension of community foundations' missions.

The added value of nonprofit/nongovernmental organizations and private philanthropy to community partnerships is central in the experience of the partnerships featured herein. It is important to understand these dynamics because community partnerships will be crucial to solving problems in the future, and the effectiveness of community partnerships depends on private philanthropy and nonprofit/nongovernmental organizations. This does not mean that government is not significant. Government, to varying degrees, remains the most important tool to address the public's interests. But local governments need help from other partners. The different international contexts of this book feature partnerships demonstrating the relative capacity of local governments. Many of these partnerships are operating in context with relatively miniscule nongovernmental sectors. The common good, in many countries, is vastly government's domain. Certainly, in the U.S. context, government does not play as significant a role in community partnerships. However, some of these dynamics are changing in other parts of the world, as private philanthropy and the nonprofit/nongovernmental sector continues to grow internationally.

Finally, the private sector is where wealth is generated. There is not a total separation between the private sector and private philanthropy, which plays a significant role in financing the nonprofit/nongovernmental sector. But while public/private partnerships that bring corporations into creative transactions with government have received considerable attention, community partnerships involving the public, private, and nonprofit/nongovernmental organizations and philanthropy require further exploration. Indeed, corporate social responsibility is a robust field with a lengthy history. But corporate programs alone have not proven to be as impactful as some may have hoped. Corporate engagement within community partnerships intending to strengthen localities could be an important pathway to leveraging corporate resources for societal gain. The evolving role of the nonprofit/nongovernmental sector and private philanthropy presents an opportunity to collectively involve foundations, universities, hospitals, museums, community-based organizations, corporations, government, and others in viable community partnerships that can improve health, education, the economy, the environment, public safety, and a variety of concerns that tend to be manifested locally.

# NOTES

1. I discuss the role of strategy in partnerships at greater length in *Strategic Public Private Partnerships* (Maurrasse, 2013).
2. In New York City, the impact of coronavirus has been disproportionately concentrated in *lower-income neighborhoods* and *communities of color*. Black New Yorkers are two times more likely to die from COVID-19 than their white counterparts; Hispanic New Yorkers are 1.8 times more likely. Similar racial and socioeconomic inequalities have been seen in outbreaks across the country.
3. The social determinants of health are the conditions in which people are born, grow, live, work, and age. These circumstances are shaped by the distribution of money, power, and resources at global, national, and local levels. The social determinants of health are mostly responsible for health inequities – the unfair and avoidable differences in health status seen within and between countries.
4. The Economic Policy Institute (Bivens & Shierholz, 2020) estimated in March 2020 that a relief and recovery package would need to be at least $2.1 trillion just through the end of 2020, and noted that this was the number for a package that was well targeted and would reliably deliver the vast majority of benefits to workers and their families. Even though it included more than $2 trillion in funding, key design failures indicated the legislation would not be large enough to provide the necessary economic relief and recovery. The economy would continue to operate significantly below potential through the end of the year, even in optimistic scenarios where the shock caused by social distancing measures is relatively short.
5. A study (Pollock, et al., 2019) in the *American Journal of Public Health* revealed that preventive coordination of community members, faith-based organizations, nonprofits, academic institutions, hospitals, police, public health services, neighborhood associations, and government agencies contributes to planning and response systems that react to *disasters* quickly, equitably, and effectively.
6. The *unemployment rate* in the U.S. stood at 11.1% as of June. While this is a marked improvement from the 14.7% jobless rate in April, it is still higher than at any time in at least the last 70 years. In some U.S. cities – many of which are major economic hubs – the unemployment crisis is far worse than it is nationwide.
7. The announcements of government containment and health-care policies lead to increases in stock market returns. Further, better containment and health policies are likely to produce benefits in terms of lower new infections and mortality rates. Lower mortality rates in turn provide enormous economic benefits in terms of more saved lives.

# 3. The nongovernmental sector and philanthropy

The nonprofit sector in the U.S. is very robust and continuing to grow.[1] The sector (also known as the nongovernmental sector, the third sector, the independent sector, or the social sector) is incredibly diverse. It includes very small community-based organizations and large think tanks. It includes small private colleges, community colleges, and large research universities. It includes hospitals, museums, libraries, community development corporations, and a variety of types of organizations of varying sizes. All of these organizations are driven by a social mission. They exist with a public purpose, and their "owners" are volunteers, who hold the organization in trust of a local government (state level in the U.S. context).

Their social missions make these organizations important players in a societal landscape. They are neither government nor private business. They essentially represent civil society. Some nonprofit organizations are specifically designed to advocate for particular populations. Different types of nonprofits play varying roles in their communities. Hospitals and universities operate in ways that are reflective of their industries. These methods of operation might be distinct from a nonprofit service provider or a community center. The budget sizes of nonprofit organizations vary substantially. This reality also shapes the differential experiences of nonprofit organizations. A well-endowed university or hospital or even a think tank with a substantial budget experience their realities and communities differently.

Because nonprofits depend upon philanthropy, larger nonprofit organizations with significant budgets operate with a direct relationship to existing wealth. Smaller, grassroots nonprofit organizations might depend upon smaller philanthropic contributions and voluntarism to function. These smaller organizations, particularly those that are neighborhood-based and neighborhood-focused, might more accurately reflect the perspectives and interests of their local constituents. These community-based nonprofit organizations, therefore, play a vital role in their local communities and, in some ways, reflect the essence of the intended role of the nonprofit sector as a third sector alongside government and the private sector. The importance of nonprofit organizations as agents of civil society is their ability to represent, and reflect, public interests. While government embodies the public sector, the broader population requires continuous representation. Governments can reflect the priorities of public officials and policymakers, and sometimes not adequately serve constituents. In this regard, nonprofit organizations that truly reflect constituents can hold both the public and private sectors accountable. The symbiosis across the three sectors, ideally, can ensure ways to meet the public's needs.

One of the great challenges to this potential ongoing added value of nonprofit organizations in society is inequality. Inequities come in many forms – economics, race, gender, and other factors. The pursuit of equity at the community level requires the full attention of the three sectors, and a range of types of nonprofit organizations, including philanthropy. In most societies, equity does not tend to emerge automatically. It is often public advocacy that influences more equitable policies and practices. As the COVID-19 pandemic and the rising awareness of persistent racial and other inequities have highlighted the breadth of social and economic disparities, how can civil society, the nonprofit, public, and private sectors collaboratively influence significant change? Within such a framework, nonprofit organizations of all types and sizes would have to not only participate, but also play catalytic roles.

With the growth of nonprofit organizations, some institutions have become significant employers and economic actors in local communities. Universities and hospitals in many urban areas have become the largest local employers.[2] These entities have become *anchor institutions* because they tend to remain in their localities and play a vital role in their communities and economies. Their economic impact can be substantial,[3] in some instances driving local economies. Many of the local communities in which private corporations were once the largest employers now rely more heavily on large nonprofit organizations. Overall, the nonprofit sector comprises a significant percentage of the U.S. labor market.[4] Beyond the U.S., the nonprofit sector continues to grow[5] and has continually expanded since the second half of the twentieth century.[6] Growth in other parts of the world is more recent. It is representative of the changing role of government, but also the recognition of the power of independent nongovernmental voices. Growth in nonprofit organizations is not merely a matter of filling the void left by shrinking government. It also demonstrates a need for representative voices beyond government. Governments can become authoritarian. Governments can change based on the party in power.

Community-based nonprofit organizations represent residents in neighborhoods, and pay attention to their particular needs. Actually, most nonprofits are small and community-based, serving local needs: 92% spend less than $1 million annually; 88% spend less than $500,000 (National Council of Nonprofits, 2019). At the community level, residents experience life – their health, their schools, their transportation, their safety, and more. They need organizations that will represent their interests consistently. The idea of creating and incorporating a nonprofit organization to reflect community priorities has become an important tool for social change. Communities are increasingly relying on nonprofit organizations for vital services. Certain services are probably best situated in government, but where service gaps exist, nonprofits can fill them. Community-based nonprofit organizations can also advocate on behalf of their constituents. They can serve as liaisons to their constituents to larger organizations in their localities as well.

While universities and hospitals might represent one end of the nonprofit sector, and community-based nonprofits serving grassroots constituents might reflect another, it is important to note the variation among larger anchor institutions. A university with a small endowment that enrolls lower-income students, who are mostly people of color, has a similar, but largely distinct experience compared with a well-endowed university that largely enrolls students from wealthy backgrounds that pay expensive tuition fees. A hospital that serves patients regardless of an ability to pay versus a hospital that largely serves the wealthy also experiences a different reality. These entities are *community-centric anchor institutions*.

These anchor institutions depend on largely underserved populations for their survival. They exist in a directly interdependent relationship with constituents in their localities that are adversely impacted by persistent disparities. During the pandemic, lower-income college students were adversely affected by the transition to remote learning. They needed computers, access to the internet, off-campus meals, dedicated quiet rooms for working at home, and any variety of resources that are common to wealthier populations. As lower-income populations disproportionately contracted COVID-19, they went to the hospitals in the communities that tend to serve their families and neighbors. In both of these instances, community-centric anchor institutions were placed in the position of providing additional services to their already vulnerable constituents. These institutions maintain a built-in commitment to populations that are confronted with many challenges. Therefore, they have a particular role to play in community partnerships that intend to reduce inequities and stimulate greater equity.

Whether large employers or small community-based organizations, nonprofits are and can be fundamental to local economies and societies.[7] They can provide connective tissue in fractured contexts. When this type of nonprofit in a locality collaborates with government and the private sector, community partnerships arise. This form of collaboration has been validated during the pandemic, as many communities required cross-sector coordination in order to navigate a changing and disruptive set of circumstances. But given the significance of nonprofit organizations to effective multistakeholder community partnerships, it is important to focus attention particularly on philanthropy. Not only does philanthropy help drive the nonprofit sector, it also brings uniquely valuable resources that enable community-based collaboration.

# PRIVATE PHILANTHROPY AND LOCAL COMMUNITIES

Alongside the expansion of the nonprofit/nongovernmental sector is the growth of private philanthropy.[8] These developments are intertwined. Private philanthropy has enabled nonprofits to grow and develop. But, because philanthropy is an extension of wealth creation, it is fraught with power dynamics. Increasingly, philanthropy is under scrutiny about the role and control of foundations and donors in relation to the most underserved populations. Philanthropic resources are sorely needed at the community level, particularly considering recent public health and economic developments.

Issues of power and control in philanthropy are central to understanding the potential and limitation of foundations' and donors' roles in facilitating change at the local level and beyond. In community partnerships, private philanthropy can play various roles, but donors and foundations should not make all of the decisions simply because they bring money to the table. Various forms of philanthropy that intend to reduce disproportionate levels of control are being explored,[9] such as participatory grantmaking and trust-based philanthropy. It seems the range of ways that philanthropy has been exploring paths to involving external constituents in decision making could be considered *community driven philanthropy*.

This notion is particularly significant with respect to community partnerships. If foundations and donors want to influence how community-based organizations, anchor institutions, the private and public sectors collaborate in their localities, they would have to do so with humility. They would have to listen to local constituents and be willing to allow the uses of their resources to be influenced by local needs and interests. Power dynamics in local communities are important to consider across the board,[10] because they are evident in how all larger institutions interface with local populations, especially lower-income constituents and communities of color. Guiding values and principles can play a crucial role in shaping how philanthropy and larger institutions in other fields approach community partnerships. For example, the Anchor Institutions Task Force subscribes to a few values that should be pursued in community partnerships: a commitment to place, equity and social justice, democracy and democratic practice, and collaboration.[11]

In localities, philanthropy's role has been evolving. Community foundations are *anchor institutions* in themselves, not only as stable local assets, but as entities with a mission focused specifically on the well-being of their communities. Community foundations have been vehicles to gather resources from donors interested in a particular geographic area in a central hub. The community foundation model in itself is also growing in the U.S. and around the world.[12] Community foundations and other locally focused philanthropic institutions have been playing a vital role in the development, expansion, and enhancement of community partnerships, as is demonstrated in the experiences of community partnerships featured herein.

While philanthropy is growing around the world, it is a much larger industry in the U.S. Across 39 countries, 260,000 institutional foundations are in existence.[13] But these are largely concentrated in Europe and North America. Among a global aggregate total of $1.5 trillion, roughly 60% is concentrated in the U.S. and about 37% is in Europe.[14] Moreover, the majority of these foundations were created in the last 25 years. This is telling in a landscape that has a significant impact on how community partnerships are manifested in the U.S., Europe, and around the world. If philanthropy is a catalytic asset helping to create and maintain community partnerships, then the concept of community partnership is differentially positioned in the U.S. and Europe in comparison to the rest of the world.

However, as demonstrated in a couple of the partnerships featured in this book, U.S. foundations can have an impact on community partnerships in lower-income developing nations. The expansion of philanthropy around the world demonstrates a realization of the potential of private capital to fill voids that government cannot fully address, but also a recognition of the potential innovative benefits that can derive from leveraging flexible private funds in order to develop and strengthen nongovernmental organizations that represent voices and perspectives across various segments in civil society. The experiences of some of the partnerships profiled herein demonstrate some of the benefits that philanthropy can bring to creative local problem solving.

In community partnerships, resources from private philanthropy can be crucial. There is no single model for financing these collaborative initiatives. Some sustain their work through membership dues from partners. Some rely on a central organization – a nonprofit or a consulting firm – to raise money to manage the partnership. Whatever the format, private philanthropy can bring important assets to community partnerships. Beyond financial resources, private foundations can bring credibility to a community partnership. A foundation can help bring partners together. Some community partnerships are coordinated by community foundations. Some foundations have initiated community partnerships. For foundations that are locally focused, community partnerships can help fulfil a program agenda. Even beyond locally focused foundations, some philanthropic institutions focused nationally or globally pursue site-based funding, realizing that it is easier to demonstrate impact by focusing funding in localities.

All of the partnerships featured in this book involve philanthropy in some way. Part II explores a variety of manifestations of community partnerships in U.S. and international contexts, capturing the role of nonprofit organizations and philanthropy in these efforts. What can we learn from these attempts to solve problems in localities by leveraging multiple local institutions? How are these partnerships able to become agents of change in their geographic areas? How have nonprofits and philanthropy facilitated their ability to strengthen their communities? Ultimately, these are important inquiries as we consider the tools that will be required to help communities navigate troubling times and an uncertain future.

## NOTES

1.  From 2006 to 2016, the number of nonprofit organizations registered with the Internal Revenue Service rose from 1.48 million to 1.54 million, an increase of 4.5 %. These 1.54 million organizations comprise a diverse range of nonprofits, including art, health, education, and advocacy nonprofits; labor unions; and business and professional associations (Urban Institute, 2020).
2.  Over half (55%) of all nonprofit jobs in the U.S. are in the health-care field. Hospitals account for the bulk of these jobs, employing 34% of the nation's total nonprofit workforce, or roughly one out of every three nonprofit workers. Health clinics and nursing homes account for the additional 21%. Fourteen percent of all nonprofit jobs in the U.S. are in educational services, including private elementary and secondary schools, colleges, universities, and other educational facilities (Salamon and Newhouse, 2019).
3.  According to the National Center for Charitable Statistics, Urban Institute (2020), the nonprofit sector contributed an estimated $1.047.2 trillion to the U.S. economy in 2016, composing 5.6 % of the country's gross domestic product.
4.  Economists regularly consider any industry or economic sector that employs 5% of a country's workforce to be a "major" industry or sector. It is therefore notable that the 12.3 million paid workers employed by U.S. nonprofit establishments as of 2016 accounted for a substantial 10.2% of the total U.S. private workforce.
5.  Based on longitudinal data of nonprofit institutions in 12 EU countries, the third or social economy sector has recently been in the midst of significant growth in these countries – growing at a rate that exceeds the growth of overall employment in the economy. Furthermore, the Australian nonprofit sector has maintained a steady growth rate as well. Over the last 20 years, the income growth has been strong at 8.4% and the rate of growth in employee numbers has been 3.7% annually, bringing the total to a significant 8.5% of the Australian workforce plus another 3% if volunteers are included (Salamon & Sokolowski, 2016).
6.  According to Statista Research Department (2021), the total number of nonprofit organizations in the U.S. has increased from 1.16 million in 1998 to 1.54 million in 2016; while total assets of reporting public charities in the U.S. has dramatically increased from $1.43 trillion to $3.79 trillion during the same period.
7.  According to the National Council of Nonprofits (2019), there are 12.3 million nonprofit employees and more than 64 million nonprofit board members and other volunteers across the U.S.
8.  Americans gave $449.64 billion in 2019. This reflects a 5.1% increase from 2018. American corporate giving in 2019 increased to $21.09 billion – a 13.4% increase from 2018. American foundation giving in 2019 increased to $75.69 billion – a 2.5% increase from 2018. Additionally, a study conducted by researchers at

Harvard Kennedy School (Johnson, 2018) gathered information from 260,358 philanthropic foundations in 38 countries and Hong Kong, revealing that while many countries and cultures have long traditions of philanthropic giving, the current global philanthropic foundation sector is growing. Nearly three-quarters (72%) of identified foundations were established in the last 25 years.

9.  A book that I authored, *Philanthropy and Society* (2020), specifically explores the ways in which various types of foundation have been engaging intended beneficiary populations in shaping their strategic priorities.

10. In Maurrasse (2001), I explored the power dynamics in higher education/community partnerships.

11. www.margainc.com/aitf/.

12. Community foundations have participated in the growth of international giving by U.S. foundations in recent years, with international giving by community foundations more than tripling, from $103 million in 2011 to $315 million in 2015, and community foundations' share of overall international giving by U.S. foundations more than doubling, from 1.4 percent in 2011 to 3.4 percent in 2015 (Council on Foundations, 2021).

13. https://cpl.hks.harvard.edu/files/cpl/files/global_philanthropy_report_final_april _2018.pdf.

14. https://cpl.hks.harvard.edu/files/cpl/files/global_philanthropy_report_final_april _2018.pdf.

# PART II

# Community partnerships in the United States

# 4.  Introduction to Part II

The substantial and growing nonprofit sector in the U.S. helps to define the context for the presence and proliferation of community partnerships. Philanthropic institutions in the form of various types of foundations – private foundations, family foundations, community foundations, and others – play a vital role in the development and evolution of community-based collaborative initiatives. These forms of collaboration bring together various organizations across local ecosystems of institutions to jointly seek solutions to any range of issues or problems.

The notion of *anchor institutions* has been particularly significant in these efforts. While conceptions of public–private partnerships emphasize the role of large corporations in collaboration with government, the idea of anchor institutions highlights longevity in place among various organizations that tend to remain in their geographic locations over extended periods; these include large nonprofit organizations. Universities and hospitals are most often viewed as anchor institutions. These nonprofit entities, in contemporary economies, are often among the largest local employers.

Whereas factories or retail businesses might have been the largest local employers in earlier generations, shifts in industry altered the landscape. The shift toward a knowledge economy and the movement of many corporations overseas in pursuit of lower operating costs left other types of organizations behind in localities. Growth in industries such as health care and technology along with the need to train and educate for an evolving economy molded the state of local economies even further.

Beyond higher education and health care, other types of organizations can be considered anchor institutions as well, such as museums, performing arts centers, libraries, community foundations, and others. These entities might not be large employers comparable to a research university or a major hospital, but they are embedded in the fabric of local ecosystems. With continued growth in philanthropy and the nonprofit sector as a whole, we can also find a vast array of community-based nonprofit organizations in localities. These are the organizations that are poised to represent civil society – serving and advocating on behalf of residents.

Private corporations still play a significant role in local ecosystems. As noted, many corporations are focused on their bottom line, tending to seek lower costs and higher profits, but some corporations are committed to their localities beyond financial interests. Anchor institutions are rooted in communities. For a university with extensive acres of land, moving is a complicated proposition, which is likely not profitable. Many corporations have proven to be mobile, demonstrating less commitment to remain in a locality. They often seek tax breaks in order to remain in an area or move. But some corporations are philosophically committed to their localities and regions. Therefore, they may not be as objectively rooted as some other organizations, however, they can subjectively opt to become anchor institutions.

Beyond large corporations, the most common private enterprises in local communities are small businesses. The restaurants, boutiques, delis, beauty shops, barber shops, and other businesses in neighborhoods, towns, and cities large and small are integral to daily life. This aspect of local ecosystems has been particularly damaged by the COVID-19 pandemic. These businesses tend to demonstrate the character and distinctiveness of communities. The future of small business development and stability will be among the priorities many community partnerships will be challenged to address beyond the pandemic.

Local governments are responsible for the neighborhoods, cities, towns, and counties in which these ecosystems of organizations are situated. In some instances, the interface between local government and various local organizations is obligatory or transactional. But, as the concept of community partnerships becomes a more central aspect of local governance, active engagement between local government and a blend of local organizations is becoming more common. As illustrated in the COVID-19 era, the complex challenges confronting local communities requires direct and sustained coordination and collaboration across sectors.

This is the reality that has given rise to the community partnerships profiled herein. These five examples of U.S.-based community partnerships represent a few different approaches to solving local problems through collaboration. It is important to note that these initiatives are operating in contexts characterized by substantial social and economic inequities. Community partnerships are challenged to solve problems in a way that benefits the most underserved populations in their localities. While these efforts are place-based and place-oriented, they must ensure that the needs of the people in those settings are adequately addressed.

# 5.   The Newark Anchor Collaborative

The Newark Anchor Collaborative (NAC) represents a community partnership that is significantly cross-sector, representing multiple fields. It not only includes numerous institutional members – more than a typical partnership of this sort, it is a unique blend of nonprofit organizations alongside private corporations that intend to remain in Newark for the long run. Newark has experienced significant challenges over the years, including the loss of numerous residents, limiting the local tax base. The city is characterized by significant inequities in health, education, income, and other areas. The racial dimension of these inequities is especially apparent. NAC developed within this context, and convened numerous local anchor institutions to join together and align with local government in order to bring about various solutions that can strengthen the local economy, reduce disparities, and expand long-term opportunities for the most vulnerable populations in and around Newark.

## BACKGROUND

### Background on the Partnership

NAC is an action-oriented think tank comprised of private and public institutional leaders from multiple fields and industries dedicated to the city's economic revitalization (Newark Alliance, 2020a). It is housed at the Newark Alliance, a leading nonprofit organization working towards the ongoing economic revitalization of Newark (Newark Alliance, 2020b). Since 2004, the Newark Alliance has received a number of grants from both public and private sources to facilitate its mission of workforce development. A 2018 grant from JPMorgan Chase to expand the CareerWorks program has fed directly into the development of the NAC (Newark Alliance, 2021a). In this way, JPMorgan Chase became a key financial partner in NAC's creation.

NAC's founding institutional partners include Prudential (the primary philanthropic contributor), Broadridge Financial, City of Newark, Edison Properties, Essex County College, Horizon Blue Cross Blue Shield, MCJ Amelior Foundation, New Jersey Institute of Technology, New Jersey Performing Arts Center, New Jersey Symphony Orchestra, Panasonic, RBH Group, Rutgers Biomedical and Health Sciences, Rutgers University-Newark, and Robert Wood Johnson Barnabas. This partnership is unique in that nonprofits are co-existing in a collaboration with various private corporations. Prudential and Rutgers University-Newark are the co-chairs of NAC. These anchor institutions are coming together around a common interest in the future of their locality. As these institutions are within the Newark area, they are inter-dependent with the conditions of the city. Each partner brings unique resources to the table and shares in a common vision for equitable development in the city where they all share headquarters. While their work addresses a number of other aspects of life in Newark including health, NAC's initial work focused on strengthening the local economy through local hiring and procurement as well as encouraging the institutions' employees to live in the city of Newark. While many significant employers are based in Newark, employees at these institutions do not necessarily live in the city. While considered a place to work, Newark is not necessarily viewed as a desirable place to live.

The focus on the local economy is very much related to the interdependence that these varied institutional partnerships share. They have a vested interest in doing business in a thriving locality. NAC is simultaneously significantly conscious of the importance of striving for equitable local economic develop-ment. Therefore, NAC is focusing both on the place of Newark as well as on its people, especially lower-income people of color. Remaining wary of local economic development initiatives that have led to gentrification and displace-ment among lower-income populations, NAC focuses on equitable growth and racial equity.

Currently, NAC is comprised of 17 anchor institutions, each of which sends a representative to the NAC table and shares learnings on the institutions' respective efforts to hire local residents, purchase from local businesses, attract new residents, address the COVID-19 pandemic, and pursue racially equita-ble policies and practices. NAC meets quarterly, and includes a number of "working groups" that meet continuously. NAC is co-chaired by the president of Rutgers University-Newark and the president of the Prudential Foundation. Additionally, a consulting firm, Marga Incorporated,[1] acts as a *learning partner*. Marga supplements NAC's work, providing insights into trends regarding anchor community partnerships – nationally and internationally – sharing ideas and offering direction for navigating economic development as an anchor collaborative.[2] Marga helped NAC design its programming and structure and continues to serve as a strategic advisor in order to enhance their effectiveness. Among the founding institutions Broadridge Financial, Horizon Blue Cross Blue Shield, New Jersey Institute of Technology, New Jersey Performing Arts Center, Prudential, Robert Wood Johnson Barnabas Health, and Rutgers University-Newark remain in NAC. They have been joined by Audible, the Newark Museum of Art, Mars, Inc., Public Service Enterprise Group, United Airlines, and University Hospital, all of whom are headquar-tered in Newark and members of the Newark Alliance. NAC acts as a community of practice, which provides a forum for knowledge sharing and joint strategizing led by directors and program coordinators from relevant departments within the member institutions. Its leadership structure harnesses expertise from different dimensions of economic development, bringing together perspectives from higher education as well as from philanthropy, health care, and the private sector.[3] In this way NAC comprehensively discusses aspects of well-being for Newark residents in its strategic approach.

### Geographical, Historical, and Cultural Context

Throughout the late nineteenth and early twentieth centuries Newark residents were primarily involved in agricultural and industrial economic activity, including construction. These sectors saw favorable growth during the years of the First World War. However, the Great Depression marked the start of a significant economic downturn in Newark.[4] Intermittent public works projects at the time could not alleviate the acute suffering in New Jersey towns where rampant pay cuts, shift reductions, and firings forced approximately 600,000 into destitution.[5] Established in 1932 to coordinate support for New Jersey residents, the New Jersey Emergency Administration was dismantled after just four years due to rapidly depleted funding for the program (Guarino, 2014). Hardship for Newark residents continued through the Second World War, despite the temporary wartime boost in employment opportunities for many people.

Demographic and economic shifts during the mid-twentieth century have shaped contemporary Newark, situating NAC's efforts to improve livelihoods in the city. In the postbellum south, the oft glossed-over years of reconstruction saw the establishment of Black Codes – and subsequent Jim Crow laws – that maintained severe restrictions on the movement of newly freed Black Americans for decades. Millions of Black people relocated from the southern states to northern ones between 1930 and 1970 in pursuit of improved living conditions and opportunities. These populations moved to cities in particular, including Newark. Simultaneously, white residents of Newark increasingly abandoned the city center. In what is commonly known as "white flight," white people were moving out of cities and bringing their established wealth with them to suburban areas.[6] During the Great Depression just 20 years prior, municipal budgets were crippled due to sharp declines in local property tax revenue and in real estate prices overall (New Jersey Almanac, n.d.). White flight caused a repeat in these conditions in Newark, hampering the municipal budget and business activity. In a report published in 1959, a group of Newark business leaders affiliated with Rutgers acknowledged that "postwar *flight to the suburbs*" was particularly marked in the Greater Newark Area (Business Executives' Research Committee, 1959, 22–28). Economic growth in the metropolitan area slowed. The Great Migration and white flight coincided in Newark, as observed in major cities across the northeast region, giving rise to an increasingly racially diverse metropolitan area with diminishing resources.

Overall population decline in the core of the Greater Newark Area persisted as internal migration to areas around the core city, whose congested industrial features and expanding racial and ethnic diversity prompted additional departures, particularly by white residents (Business Executives' Research Committee, 1959, 27). Furthermore, gradual decline – or relocation – of the industrial sector left many newcomers to Newark without the manufacturing and construction jobs that had been the hallmark of the Newark economy for decades.[7]

These trends help to explain the emphasis placed on workplace development since the early days of the Newark Alliance. The Newark Alliance was founded by leaders from major New Jersey corporations in order to support the broad needs of the Newark community. Since its inception in 1999, the Newark Alliance has worked to create partnerships with key stakeholders in order to address critical issues and advance Newark's economic revitalization as well as its public education.[8]

Presently, NAC continues decades of work responding to the demographic and economic shifts seen in Newark during the middle of the twentieth century. Business and community leaders in Newark have long been dedicated to supporting residents in achieving better health outcomes and improved economic conditions.

NAC is the latest in a long line of successful initiatives by the Newark Alliance and its partners aimed at improving lives in the community. The Newark Alliance envisions Newark as a "regional city," serving as an economic and cultural hub in the region.[9] The economic dimension of this vision is particularly salient to the local government. Newark's mayor Ras Baraka prioritized economic development in the "Newark 2020" effort of the Hire.Buy. Live.Newark Initiative.[10] A primary objective of Newark 2020 is to connect 2,020 unemployed Newark residents to quality employment opportunities by the end of the 2020 calendar year. Newark, the largest city in New Jersey, has seen an unemployment rate higher than the state level. Reducing this rate of joblessness has become a target for the city government and for groups like the Newark Alliance and the Initiative for a Competitive Inner City, both of whom have helped to shape the Newark 2020 plan.

## STRATEGY

### Primary Initiatives

Hire.Buy.Live Local is the key component for NAC. NAC members have committed to advancing one dimension of this flagship program. Each member capitalizes on its own expertise and resources to address the hire, buy, or live aspect. Thus, the level of engagement around the three workstreams varies but there is shared commitment. Within the past year and a half, NAC members have emphasized racial equity as an element of primary programming in the network. Racial equity work is emerging as a signature project for NAC. Race transcends strategies to increase local hiring and purchasing as well as approaches to expand the number of local residents. The advent of the COVID-19 pandemic and the national racial reckoning that gained momentum during the summer of 2020 only underscored the importance of NAC's racial equity signature project.

Because Hire.Buy.Live Local is such a central program, NAC has established a working group for each of the three dimensions with its own director. As NAC members engage in their work around Hire.Buy.Live Local they coordinate with the relevant director. NAC recently established a racial equity working group as well. Strategically, NAC is contributing to strengthening the local economy by aligning with the City of Newark and the Newark Alliance. They have created a forum that allows local anchor institutions that employ and purchase to target these functions in order to expand opportunities for local residents. Given that local economic development strategies can run the risk of displacing or overlooking the most vulnerable populations, NAC is consciously helping its members develop and refine racially equitable policies and practices. Using a learning exchange approach within a community of practice, NAC helps members learn from each other's experiences.

Quarterly NAC meetings serve as opportunities to report on progress in each of the three dimensions of Hire.Buy.Live Local and to share wins as well as challenges with regard to the work. This format is conducive to mutual learning and capacity building. The members help each other meet Hire.Buy.Live goals and become more racially equitable institutions.

NAC coordinates with the City of Newark, particularly on the Live Local program which has been shaped through combined effort. The city government has its own housing incentives program comprised of external grants to homeowners to help cover the cost of exterior home improvements. Live Local mirrors the city's initiative. A previous project director restructured Live Local to mirror the city initiative (how the program operated and how applications were received). Beyond coordination with Newark's local government, the anchor institutions help to implement Live Local. City counselors also provide NAC with insights into connecting with constituents and identifying potential applicants to the flagship program. NAC routinely reports to the City on the volume of applications.

**Funding the Work**

Since NAC's inception, Prudential has been instrumental in catalyzing anchor work in Newark. In 2015, the Initiative for a Competitive Inner City (ICIC) published a report (Ferguson and Zeuli, n.d.) on Buy Local that engaged all of the anchors at the table. ICIC is a national not-for-profit organization that aims to encourage inner-city revitalization. It performs research that promotes a combination of public and private investment to rebuild inner-city econo-mies (Community Wealth, 2020). The report was based on a study funded by Prudential. Following the report, the group of anchors involved in the study continued to meet and further coordinate efforts on economic development in Newark. In this way, Prudential brought together a group of anchor insti-tutions that otherwise would likely not have engaged with one another to the same degree of collaboration as they have through NAC. Prudential played a significant role in laying the groundwork for NAC by bringing together these anchors with an agenda oriented toward improving economic conditions in the city. Currently, Prudential remains an influential partner in NAC, supporting many initiatives, including financial contributions.

Hire.Buy.Live aims to dramatically reduce poverty and unemployment and to strengthen the city's economy through three integrated strategies. Partners in the initiative include: Audible, City of Newark, Edison Properties, Horizon, the Institute, Local Initiatives Support Corporation, Maher Terminals, NAC, New Jersey Institute of Technology, Newark Alliance, Newark Community Development Network, Panasonic, Port Newark Container Terminal, Ports America, Prudential Center, Public Service Enterprise Group, Robert Wood Johnson Barnabas, Rutgers Biomedical and Health Sciences, Rutgers-Newark, United Airlines, Urban League of Essex County, Verizon, and Victoria Foundation.[11]

NAC's strategy of Hire Newark aims to connect 2,020 of the city's unem-ployed to full-time living wage jobs by the year 2020, cutting in half the employment gap between Newark and New Jersey as a whole. This goal has been achieved. Buy Newark intends to support the growth of local businesses and match them to the purchasing needs of other Newark businesses large and small, including the anchors, which are committed to increasing overall local procurement by 2020.[12]

Live Newark aims to attract more employees, faculty, and students to live in the city and to provide existing residents with additional rental and homeownership choices and incentives. New Jersey Institute of Technology, New Jersey Performing Arts Center, Rutgers Biomedical and Health Sciences, and Rutgers University-Newark join Prudential as the primary partners involved with the Live Local initiative. Each of these anchors has invested in the program.[13] NAC is providing options for ways in which local anchor institutions can contribute to meeting a range of goals. As many of these goals were designed with a deadline of the end of 2020, NAC is going to embark on a process to identify new goals and timelines.

The presence of the pandemic, which began to be felt directly in Newark in March 2020, forced NAC and many other initiatives to adapt. In-person engagement, for example, was a fundamental component of NAC's community of practice, particularly in quarterly meetings. NAC converted the meetings to a virtual format. The process has worked well, and likely even increased attendance. But the reality of COVID-19 created many new challenges, as it devastated Newark in public health and economically. It also worsened many existing inequities.

## COVID-19 REALITIES

Newark has felt the health-related and economic ramifications of the pandemic more than many other cities in New Jersey. In addition to the more evident medical and health-care challenges that the virus has presented in Newark, it has also disproportionately affected Black residents. Using age-adjusted case, hospitalization, and mortality rates, New Jersey's Black and Latinx residents have suffered directly from COVID-19 at double to triple the rates of the state's white and Asian residents.[14] Program constituents are challenged with either long-term or temporary loss of employment due to the partial shutdown of the city, and globally. Residents are also facing issues related to transportation, as many of those fortunate to still have jobs are finding it difficult to get to work on a daily basis. Heightened concerns around safety and well-being are a hallmark of the COVID-19 reality. Some employers are better equipped than others when it comes to protecting workers. Even worse, some employers are taking the pandemic more seriously than others much to the dismay of Newark workers. The economic repercussions of the pandemic have hit Newark particularly hard due to its large small-business community. The majority of Newark's 13,515 businesses are relatively small; 62% of them have fewer than five employees while 70% report less than $1 million in annual revenues.[15] Business operations of small magnitude are often less resilient against economic downturn.

The COVID-19 pandemic has also affected housing conditions across Newark including the Live Local program. Candidates for the program have encountered a number of hurdles, such as very limited property showings and halts to in-person lease signings, which is a requirement for the program.

The anchors are adapting to the new work conditions imposed by a global quarantine. This includes navigating the technological challenges to engaging employers working from their respective homes, potentially across geographies and time zones. While many elements of the work can be adapted to a virtual working environment, such a transition is more logistically fraught for other aspects of the work done by anchors within NAC. This is a new reality for them. Depending on the industry, the pandemic dramatically altered how the anchor institutions do their work. One anchor within NAC, the New Jersey Performing Arts Center, was forced to halt its production season in response to the pandemic.[16] The shutdown disrupted planned programming and contributions by the New Jersey Performing Arts Center to NAC (as is the case for anchors in other cities). The performing arts is an industry that has been substantially disrupted by COVID-19. All of the fields represented in NAC have been challenged to reimagine their functions in some way. Ultimately, COVID-19 has forced anchors to change the way that they operate, likely with long-term consequences that have influenced declines in revenue, hiring freezes, and general constraints on financial capacity to compensate workers. The combination of worsening conditions from populations standing to benefit from NAC's work and increasing vulnerability among the anchors themselves creates a pivotal combination. This blend of concerns will help define NAC's future. Currently, NAC's institutional members appear to remain committed to continuing their collective pursuits to strengthen Newark, and poised to adapt their efforts to the magnitude of the challenge ahead.

NAC members sit on various boards and working groups that advise on reopening at the city and state levels. Members continue to take full advantage of opportunities for engagement with peer institutions. Increased communication between anchors during this tumultuous time of COVID-19 and social justice uprisings has proven a precious resource to NAC as important information sharing. Convenings of members also provide an opportunity for identifying synergies between anchor work streams. For example, one anchor might share a project currently in development and then another anchor will offer a particular resource or other form of support for the project going forward. NAC is continuing to stay engaged as it advances its work virtually.

Two or three weeks into the pandemic quarantine, a colleague at Hire Local launched an emergency staffing effort through which she connected work candidates to opportunities in the health field. Quite a few anchors supported this effort acknowledging the need to meet urgent health-related needs in Newark. Anchors circulated specific opportunities for work and shared training opportunities to empower available workers to fulfill new roles. Through Marga, the Anchor Institutions Task Force, a network of leaders promoting the engagement of anchor institutions in community and economic development, is performing ongoing research on how anchor institutions are responding in their communities given COVID-19. This research has helped NAC understand the range of ways in which anchor institutions have been contributing in their communities during the pandemic beyond Newark.

In the Live Local program, applicants are having difficulty securing their leases. Applicants typically have a 45 day period during which they need to sign a lease in order to be eligible for the assistance program.[17] NAC is extending this deadline to give people more time to find housing given the extraordinary circumstances.

Anchors are also coming together on the contact tracing[18] work spearheaded by the Newark Alliance. NAC has taken the lead in creating a Newark-specific framework contact tracing implemented in partnership with the city government. Anchors are mobilizing volunteers and employees to help facilitate contact tracing in a collaborative effort to manage the spread of COVID-19.

The City of Newark and United Way have launched a joint recovery fund to address the urgent needs of Newark residents in the time of COVID-19. The City of Newark, United Way, and Invest Newark also created Newark's Small Business Emergency Grant Fund. Faculty members of Rutgers University-Newark School of Public Affairs and Administration worked with the Urban League of Essex County to assess the impact of COVID-19 by surveying Newark residents.[19]

As the pandemic has ushered in a new reality facing NAC, there is much to consider about NAC's strategic approach going forward. This unique partnership has created a model that has proven to withstand the pandemic. NAC actually added members during 2020. Overall, the work of NAC, and community partnerships, have renewed significance given recent events. NAC will have to determine how much to reshape its work in the face of the increased economic insecurity and health challenges that the pandemic will leave behind. In areas that are not directly addressed by NAC, such as education, inequities are particularly striking. This will influence the future of employment opportunities in the area. NAC will begin taking stock of the impact of the pandemic on numerous aspects of life in Newark, and determine an appropriate role for members to play in addressing them and pursuing new goals. NAC will also have to ponder the limits of its work. Perhaps the partnership will remain a community of practice that enables learning exchange among members regarding their respective efforts. But NAC could decide to add a dimension in which NAC promotes additional joint activity among members that could lead to more of a collective voice that advocates for citywide changes.

Overall, NAC has established an important foundation for the unstable future ahead. For community partnerships, transcending institutional silos, and bringing partners together around common goals is quite challenging.

Furthermore, NAC was able to connect nonprofit organizations and large private corporations around their joint interest in the future of Newark. They were also able to create a model that maintains a path of communication and cooperation with local government.

## NOTES

1. Marga Incorporated is a New York-based consulting firm providing strategic advice and research to philanthropic initiatives and community partnerships. A substantial portion of Marga's work is designed to strengthen the role of anchor institutions in community and economic development.
2. Sibusisiwe Malaba in conversation with the author, May 2020.
3. Sibusisiwe Malaba in conversation with the author, May 2020.
4. During the Great Depression, the jobless in New Jersey ranged between a quarter to a third of its workforce. New Jersey per capita income fell from $839 in 1929 to $433 in 1933 (www.newjerseyalmanac.com/great-depression-and-1930s.html).
5. https://gardenstatelegacy.com/files/Time_of_Despair_Time_of_Hope_Guarino _GSL24.pdf.
6. www.nytimes.com/1971/04/18/archives/whites-driven-by-fear-and-prejudice-flee -newark-to-suburban.html.
7. http://archive.pov.org/streetfight/newark-a-brief-history/.
8. www.newark-alliance.org/about/our-history/.
9. www.newark-alliance.org.
10. www.newark.rutgers.edu/news/2020-vision-newark-rutgers-newark-joins-other -anchors-making-hirebuylivenewark-commitments.
11. https://procurementservices.rutgers.edu/purchasing/diversity-and-sustainability/ hire-buy-live-newark.
12. https://hr.njit.edu/newark-2020-hire-buy-live-local.
13. https://procurementservices.rutgers.edu/purchasing/diversity-and-sustainability/ hire-buy-live-newark.
14. www.njpp.org/publications/report/unprecedented-and-unequal-racial-inequities -in-the-covid-19-pandemic/.
15. https://icic.org/blog/newarks-data-driven/.
16. www.njpac.org/visit/covid-health-and-safety/.
17. https://hr.njit.edu/njits-newark-live-local-program.
18. Contact tracing is a process to identify, monitor, and support individuals who may have been exposed to a person with COVID-19 (www.cdc.gov/coronavirus/2019 -ncov/community/contact-tracing-nonhealthcare-workplaces.html).
19. www.margainc.com/wp-content/uploads/2020/04/AITF-COVID-research -framework-with-examples-4.29.pdf.

# 6.  Memphis Medical District Collaborative

The Memphis Medical District Collaborative (MMDC) focuses on a particular geographic area that includes numerous anchor institutions, which are nonprofit organizations of various types and sizes – medical institutions, institutions of higher education, and philanthropic organizations. This district-focused form of community partnership tends to creatively develop initiatives around the common interests of a cluster of anchor institutions. Like the Newark Anchor Collaborative, this effort focuses on both developing the physical place in which these organizations are situated, while also creating employment and other opportunities for underserved populations. As is the case in many cities, districts of anchor institutions may exist in defined spaces with a wealth of resources while simultaneously remaining in close proximity to lower-income residents in nearby neighborhoods. It takes a conscious effort to bring these institutions together around an agenda that transcends the interests of each particular organization.

## BACKGROUND

### Background on the Partnership

MMDC is a community development organization working with partners to strengthen the communities between and around the major anchor institutions in the Memphis Medical District so that they are more livable, vibrant, and safe. It is the product of several years of collaborative strategic planning among institutional stakeholders in the medical district. Initial work to study the feasibility of an anchor strategy in the district began in May 2014 when the Hyde Family Foundation (HFF) engaged U3 Advisors[1] to study the economic impact of eight major institutions in the district: Baptist College of Health Sciences, Memphis Bioworks Foundation, Methodist/LeBonheur, Regional One Health, Southern College of Optometry, Southwest Tennessee Community College, St. Jude's Children's Research Hospital/American Lebanese Syrian Associated Charities, and the University of Tennessee Health Science Center.[2] HFF seeded the capital to initiate the exploratory research phase en route to developing an anchor strategy that made sense for Memphis. U3 Advisors brought in critical expertise from its own work on the anchor models seen in Philadelphia and midtown Detroit.

It is important to observe that the anchor institutions were ultimately encouraged to engage in community development by way of a study that was supported by a philanthropic institution, HFF. This reminds us of the catalytic role that local philanthropy can play in stimulating innovation. The U3 Advisors study that philanthropy financed helped provide the data to better understand the potential of the anchor institutions' collective resources. Economic impact studies are significant in their ability to capture the nature and scope of capital in community-based anchor institutions. But the strategic challenge to community partnerships is to determine how to leverage this knowledge in order to engage and strengthen local populations.

In the fall of 2015, eight anchors collectively committed $1.29 million to support MMDC operations and programming for the next fiscal year. A second local foundation joined HFF in November 2015, pledging $10 million over five years in philanthropic investment. The balance between financial input from anchor institutions and investment by philanthropic organizations has proven to be a successful model for a nascent anchor collaborative on this instance. At this early stage, MMDC developed a formula for calculating the amount that each anchor would contribute based largely on real estate holdings and number of employees. Today about 50% of the MMDC's funding comes from anchors based on this formula, while the other nearly 50% is from philanthropy.[3] Anchor input is gradually increasing as the collaborative weens itself off of philanthropic dollars.[4] Indeed, this is a challenge facing many community partnerships – sustaining themselves financially over time beyond grants from foundations. But, especially in the early phases of development, philanthropic resources can be simply existential. Many community partnerships, even if they are comprised of very well-resourced anchor institutions, would not be launched without philanthropy. This only reinforces why philanthropy can be absolutely pivotal in leveraging the transformation of local communities. Foundations can provide the funding that nurtures the necessary data collection and strategic thinking that helps potential partners decide on a course of action.

In its first year, MMDC's 2016 programming focused on public spaces, safety and security, programming events, community development, and anchor programs. Live Local, Buy Local, and Hire Local were initiated as original anchor programs. The Live Local program was launched with four anchor institutions and processed 200 Housing Incentive Applications in 2016. In this same year, Buy Local held seven Buy Local Purchasing Council Meetings, introduced 11 minority- or woman-owned businesses to the Buy Local Purchasing Group, and redirected more than $700,000 of new spend to local minority- or women-owned businesses. Hire Local completed a data analysis of Anchor Institution Hiring Demand and laid groundwork for the Hire Local council.[5] Today, MMDC is involved in over 20 initiatives in the district. Its programs and incentives work to strengthen neighborhoods in the district to make the area more livable, vibrant, and safe. Core programs include: Quality Public Spaces; Clean and Safe Streets; Transportation and Mobility; Live Local; Be Aware: Vision Zero Campaign; Community and Economic Development; Real-Estate; and District Events.

**Geographical, Historical, and Cultural Context**

The Memphis Medical District earned its name based on a longstanding history with medicine, beginning with the opening of the Memphis City Hospital in 1841. Today, the district is comprised mainly of institutionally owned land including several large medical campuses (Fisher-Bruns and Logan-Robinson, 2018, 9). Memphis has always been surrounded by smaller towns. The nearest major city of Nashville is a three hour drive away. Decades of urban sprawl between 1970 and 2010 led to a substantial decline in urban density contributing to overextended municipal infrastructure (Fisher-Bruns and Logan-Robinson, 2018, 9–10). Urban sprawl meant that many amenities were relocated to the outskirts of the city to which wealthier residents were relocating.

The city of Memphis is one of many cities in the southern United States to experience growth from the southwestward shift of industrial activity in the country beginning around the 1930s, partially due to unionization in the northern states (Koistinen, 2002). However, the Jim Crow Laws dramatically limited opportunities for Black people in the city. Setbacks during the era of Jim Crow set the tone for generational poverty among many Memphis residents. Inequity undermined an otherwise crucial era of economic development in the city. This has in part shaped the present economic conditions that the MMDC is working to address.

## STRATEGY

Despite investment from its institutional campuses, the district lacked the amenities that would entice workers to live there. Even today about 40% of Memphis Medical District employees are traveling at least 40 miles to and from work, including nurses commuting from rural areas to work at the hospital.[6] The primary objective of the MMDC is to enhance livability. Engaging anchors and nonprofit organizations is key to fulfilling this organizational mission.

As a community partnership, MMDC's approach centers on aggregating demand for labor, products, and services among the anchor institutions in the district. For example, the MMDC's Hire Local initiative meets institutional demand for workers by matching newly trained or transitioning workers to aggregated employment opportunities across the anchors. Hire Local, Buy Local, and Live Local programs demonstrate the MMDC's strategic approach. The purpose of these efforts is not only to maintain sustainable economic relationships involving the anchor institutions, but rather to create an environment where people of all backgrounds can thrive.

Like many community partnerships involving anchor institutions, MMDC was challenged to adapt its strategy in light of new challenges associated with the COVID-19 pandemic. At the onset of the pandemic in the U.S., MMDC conducted a SWOT analysis[7] on current projects as part of a reprioritization within the programmatic budget.

## ROLE AND VALUE OF NONGOVERNMENTAL ORGANIZATIONS AND NONPROFITS

MMDC is itself a nonprofit organization that helps to coordinate the resources and activities of large institutions in the medical district. Beyond the anchor institutions, other nonprofit organizations play a strategic role in MMDC's programming, including Advance Memphis, Center for Transforming Communities, Clean Memphis, Innovate Memphis, and Neighborhood Preservation Inc., among others.[8] These organizations play a crucial role in community development, particularly with respect to real estate development. Typically, MMDC pursues capital projects costing between $1 million and $10 million; it can be difficult to attract the necessary investment for this. These various community-based nonprofit organizations assist in shepherding such projects by making direct capital investment or by providing technical support to investors. MMDC engages nonprofit organizations on multiple levels and coordinates larger anchor institutions, which are nonprofit organizations themselves along with smaller organizations with areas of expertise particular to MMDC's programming.

## PROGRESS

MMDC released its 2019 Annual Report[9] highlighting recent accomplishments. It features initiatives such as, "Quality Public Spaces," which enhances public spaces and thoroughfares that build a stronger, safer, and more vibrant and sustainable district. Accomplishments under this initiative for 2019 include: 1.5 miles completed of the district's MLK Avenue Streetscape Enhancement Project from Peabody Avenue to 4th Street; three placemaking projects at Health Sciences Park, Edge Triangle, and Linden Park; six landscaping projects completed; six public arts projects installed. In the area of "Community and Economic Development," MMDC has been providing support services for new and existing businesses, creating retail incubation opportunities, and connecting local business procurement opportunities and residents to employment opportunities. In 2019, this work led to 10 new businesses opening in the district; 1,500 local suppliers featured in the new Buy Local Marketplace Database and three new retail bays opened as part of the Boxlot Retail Incubation Project. Their community and economic development also led to financial support for 20 businesses to improve facades and signage.

In "Real-Estate," MMDC incentives and tools have helped transform ideas into funded projects – from large-scale, transformative projects to small-scale infill developments. MMDC's real estate accomplishments in 2019 included 12 investments made in potential projects, and 11 active real estate projects. They also catalyzed and invested in a 65 unit high-quality workforce housing development. Their "Clean and Safe Streets" programming is working to ensure the safety and well-being of residents, employees, students, and visitors. This effort has led to a 112% increase in trash and recycle removal, a 100% increase in ambassador team members, and two projects supported to address homelessness through the Hospitality Hub.

MMDC's "Transportation" initiatives are connecting people to their jobs, neighborhoods, and public spaces by improving transportation and mobility options in the district. This effort has led to 200 weekly riders on the pilot launch of the Groove Shuttle, a 12 minute maximum wait for the new Groove Shuttle linking Mud Island to Memphis Medical District, and five completed mobility plans. MMDC has also developed programs connecting people to places through events that invite people to mix and experience the district. They have held over 30 events in public spaces and 12 community events in district neighborhoods to over 14,000 attendees. MMDC's "Community Engagement" includes ongoing communication with neighborhood associations, community organizations, and anchor institutions to design programs and deepen engagement with residents, employees, and students. They have organized over 30 neighborhood meetings. They have disbursed nine neighborhood grants as well. MMDC held 18 anchor institution engagement events with over 2,000 attendees. Additionally, eight neighborhoods participated in the Focus Roundtable Partnership with the Center for Transforming Communities.

The partnership responded promptly to the COVID-19 pandemic, which has exacerbated existing issues while also creating new challenges for Memphis residents. Since the onset of the pandemic, the MMDC has launched seven new initiatives aimed at response and recovery for Memphis Medical District residents and businesses. The MMDC also developed an emergency financial relief fund to provide quick support to businesses. Toward the end of the first wave of COVID-19 infections, MMDC began developing the Small Business

Mobilization Fund to facilitate reopening for businesses as well as a related effort to help restaurants prepare for safe outdoor dining.[10] Prior to COVID-19, MMDC did not engage in direct resident support. This changed after the pandemic. The Metropolitan Interfaith Association (a food bank that provides other forms of support) became a partner in helping residents make payments relating to their housing. Also, the MMDC implemented a gift card program to help residents get food and cleaning supplies during the pandemic as the world entered quarantine. Employment faltered in Memphis as a result of the economic downturn. Since the onset of COVID-19, MMDC has graduated three cohorts (10–15 residents each) through its virtual Hire Local training.

The example of MMDC in the pandemic demonstrates how an existing community partnership becomes an asset in itself. As community partnerships organize an ecosystem of existing institutions, they provide a hub for collaboration and coordination. MMDC in a crisis such as COVID-19 can, therefore, become a space for centralizing a number of necessary activities. It can become the place through which funds can be contributed and organized to support community needs, even altering its working model in order to directly support residents.

## NOTES

1. U3 Advisors works with anchor institutions to advance their mission and unlock their impact. U3 helps institutions identify shared values and take action to realize their goals for economic, physical, and cultural development (www.u3advisors .com/about-us/).
2. www.u3advisors.com/projects/memphis-medical-district-collaborative/.
3. www.mdcollaborative.org/annual-report, 27.
4. Personal communication, MMDC vice president Abby Miller, November 5, 2020.
5. https://issuu.com/mmdc901/docs/mmdc_2016annualreport.
6. Personal communication, MMDC vice president Abby Miller, November 5, 2020.
7. A SWOT analysis is a strategic planning tool for considering the strengths, weaknesses, opportunities, and threats of a particular strategy for a group and how it can be best implemented (www.betterevaluation.org/en/evaluation-options/ swotanalysis).
8. www.mdcollaborative.org/anchor-partners.
9. www.mdcollaborative.org/annual-report.
10. www.mdcollaborative.org/small-business-remobilization-fund.

# 7. Southeast Los Angeles Collaborative

The need for greater coordination of resources for community benefit is central to the work of the Southeast Los Angeles (SELA) Collaborative. This community partnership brings together a variety of nonprofit organizations that, together, are positioned to help the community navigate a series of services and activities in the local nonprofit ecosystem. An important component of this community partnership is its emphasis on civic engagement.

## BACKGROUND ON THE PARTNERSHIP

The SELA Collaborative is a network of organizations that work together to strengthen the capacity of the nonprofit sector and increase civic engagement in SELA. The SELA Collaborative was founded in 2011 by 11 core organizations. Today, it is comprised of Alliance for a Better Community, AltaMed, Council of Mexican Federations, East Los Angeles College, East Yard Communities for Environmental Justice, Families in Schools, First 5 LA, Hub Cities, Human Services Association, Pat Brown Institute at Cal State LA, Southeast Community Development Corporation, and the Southeast Rio Vista YMCA. The Collaborative focuses on three strategic areas: nonprofit capacity building, civic engagement, and data-driven research.[1]

In 2006, the Ninth Circuit Court of Appeals in Los Angeles issued a verdict decision in the case Jones v. City of Los Angeles officially decriminalizing homelessness in a move affecting the lives of around 90,000 people in Los Angeles County (American Civil Liberties Union, 2006b). Punitive city ordinances had threatened the lives of all homeless persons even as they endured dangerously high temperatures alongside their fellow Los Angeles residents. A heatwave passing through central and southern California that year set state records that would not be matched for another 14 years (Georgiou, 2020). Hundreds of people died during the heatwave, highlighting the dire need to better protect Californians, especially those without adequate shelter. The external heat matched the heightened political tensions across the country with regard to immigration policy. U.S. Representative F. James Sensenbrenner, Jr. (Republican, Wisconsin) had proposed legislation criminalizing all assistance to immigrants residing in the country without legal documentation. The proposal sparked large-scale uprisings in several cities, and some of the largest demonstrations occurred in southern California where 500,000 residents rallied in a single day in Los Angeles (Engler and Engler, 2016). Known as a common destination for immigrants from Latin America, California saw more mass mobilization against the legislation than any other state.

These events point to just some of the major issues faced by Los Angeles County communities. In the same year, community leaders began exploring how to improve the coordination of resources and services for people in need. Initial conversations helped lay the foundation for the SELA Collaborative. Five years later, in 2011, the SELA Collaborative came to fruition on the back of crucial support from the California Community Foundation, Weingart Foundation, and Ballmer Group (California Community Foundation, n.d.). The California Community Foundation granted $25,000 to jumpstart the new organization tasked with assessing civic engagement and the capacity of non-profit organizations active in the SELA area. Despite being formed in 2011, the SELA Collaborative became a truly active player in the SELA nonprofit field in 2016.

This came as a result of a successful bus tour, organized with funding received from the Weingart Foundation, and efforts by Hilda Solis.[2] The bus tour took philanthropy partners, local nonprofit leaders, council members, and residents on a tour of the SELA region. The tour celebrated the history and culture of the area, while also emphasizing what needed to be done in the region. The bus tours have advanced into the SELA Collaborative Community Tour. The tour aims to help educate about the historically under-resourced yet vital area of Los Angeles County. It also offers the opportunity for attendees to meet some of the Collaborative members working together to empower SELA communities and learn how the collaborative is addressing critical regional issues, including regionalism, social justice, equity, local accountability, and collective impact.[3] Since its early years, the SELA Collaborative has completed a community-based strategic plan, engaged additional philanthropic partners, and resumed implementing its vision and strategic plan.

## GEOGRAPHICAL, HISTORICAL, AND CULTURAL CONTEXT

The SELA Collaborative's mission is to strengthen the SELA communities, build collective power, and encourage innovation to drive regional systemic change.[4] The SELA Collaborative carries out its institutional mission across eight cities and two unincorporated areas in Los Angeles County, including Bell, Bell Gardens, Cudahy, Florence-Firestone, Huntington Park, Lynwood, Maywood, South Gate, Vernon, and Walnut Park. These communities compose a historically underserved yet vital area of Los Angeles County, and are together referred to as SELA. This region is surrounded by four different freeways: the 5 freeway to the north, the 110 freeway to the west, the 91 freeway to the south, and the 60 freeway to the north. The region is also considered part of the 710 corridor, as the 710 freeway runs through the area.[5] Each of these cities has a local council, and each one is densely populated – three of the cities are among the top ten most populous cities in the U.S.

The SELA Collaborative's target area is currently home to approximately 440,000 people. The area contains many young families and many residents are younger than the county average: 30% of the population is under the age of 18 and an additional 28% is between the ages of 18 to 34. Over 90% of the population across SELA communities identifies as Latinx. The area is also home to just over 191,000 immigrants, representing about 44% of the total population, 10% higher than the county average. The SELA region includes 126,455 noncitizen immigrants, representing just over two-thirds of the total immigrant population. Cudahy, Bell Gardens, and Florence-Firestone have the largest share of noncitizen immigrants – 74%, 73%, and 73% of their immigrant populations are noncitizens, respectively. Of children under the age of 18, approximately 5% are immigrants, nearly all of whom are noncitizens. The unemployment rate in the SELA region averages 11.01% – higher than the county average of 8.9%. The SELA community has a median household income of roughly $40,500, lower than the Los Angeles County median of almost $58,000 (Thornberg et al., 2017).

In 2017, the Pat Brown Institute for Public Affairs (a member of the collaborative) provided an analysis of the human, housing, business, and transportation assets of the SELA region as defined by the collaborative. As stated in the analysis:

> Political disunity has remained an obstacle to developing a regional voice, which is particularly disabling in a county with so many stakeholders vying for resources. This report hopes to change that by creating a unified vision of what this community is, and the assets that will play a role in its future growth (Thornberg et al., 2017).

The analysis depicted a growing community with great opportunity for continued development and positive outcomes for residents. The geographic area now commonly referred to as Southeast Los Angeles evolved into a hub of industrialization as a result of its proximity to major rail routes that served the Port of Long Beach. The region continues to maintain a strong industrial character as industries have continued to transition over time. By 1993, the industry was dominated by apparel and textiles. This trend has continued with the most recent economic expansion in the leisure, hospitality, and retail trade (Thornberg et al., 2017). In recent decades the population has continued to increase and there is a struggle for resources and continued community development.

# STRATEGY

The nature of the region, spread across multiple municipalities with great "disunity," set the state for the SELA Collaborative's strategy. As is the case with other community partnerships, the work is defined by the local context. The SELA Collaborative aims to fill a gap between the government and its residents. It is designed to increase civic engagement among residents as a pathway to their involvement in local governance.

SELA Collaborative executive director Dr. Wilma Franco believes that local governments have struggled to see the communities they represent as contributors to solutions, rather than the way they are traditionally viewed as recipients of a service. As a result, she believes that attempts by those in public office to help communities have often not attached themselves to critical issues, or have not addressed the root causes of those issues. By involving residents in the decision-making process, Franco hopes to change the way in which public officials see solutions, as "residents are not seen as experts, but they might have better solutions as they live in their everyday environment." An important dimension of this is building the capacity of community-based nonprofit organizations.

# ROLE OF NONGOVERNMENTAL ORGANIZATIONS AND NONPROFITS

The SELA Collaborative's key objective with increasing nonprofit capacity is to create a robust infrastructure of local nonprofits by building on the assets already existing within the community. SELA is working from the premise that an increase of strong nonprofit organizations in the region will strengthen the community. Nonprofits are essential in creating a unified voice to help engage both internal and external stakeholders around a shared vision for the region, helping build community assets and directly responding to individual and community-wide needs. By strengthening the ability of the nonprofit sector in SELA, the SELA Collaborative hopes to create a regional vision with the residents and organizations in the SELA region aimed at achieving health and well-being for individuals community-wide.

Nonprofits in SELA provide essential services to residents by directing services to families and children, organizing residents for social change, fostering affordable housing and community development, influencing public policies, and publishing research to elevate awareness on local issues. The collaborative aims to strengthen the SELA nonprofit sector by conducting a comprehensive assessment, increasing existing nonprofit capacity, developing human capacity by creating a pipeline of leaders, and supporting nonprofit incubation.

This community partnership is placing the nonprofit organizations that work most closely with the general population in the region at the center. These tend to be smaller organizations with far fewer resources than many larger anchor institutions. These more grassroots nonprofit organizations are community-centric, and positioned to represent the voices of their constituents somewhat uniquely. A range of these types of organizations can be found in most U.S. communities. This is a crucial aspect of the ecosystem in any neighborhood, town, city, or region. By emphasizing building the capacity of these organizations, the SELA Collaborative is shining a light on an important reality – grassroots nonprofit organizations are usually under-resourced. If they are to reach their potential as strong voices of and assets to their communities, they need greater funding as well as overall capacity – staffing, infrastructure, and more.

## FUTURE DIRECTIONS

Given the young age of the organization, the SELA Collaborative is currently at a crossroads in crafting its future intentions. According to Franco, much of the collaborative's work in 2019 was dedicated to reflection. This entails "reflecting on what needs to be done, as well as what can realistically be accomplished, and what the SELA Collaborative has the capacity to do in the future."

Franco is looking to tackle a key dilemma with the SELA Collaborative in the future: "How do we create systemic change and build collective power?" She believes that answering this question will take time and money. The collaborative is considering taking on work that is noncollaborative in nature, while also deciding on what aspects of the collaborative's mission to stress. This involves "establishing what the community wants and strengthening it, as well as finding what makes the biggest contribution."

The SELA Collaborative is currently reviewing how it can diversify its financial support streams, and is considering how it can begin to receive government funding. Franco mentions that the collaborative would like to be able to apply for government funding opportunities as they arise. In the meantime, the collaborative supports people and organizations who do apply for government funding, as well as supporting elected officials in each of the communities it serves.

Despite plans to explore diversification, Franco believes that philanthropy will continue to play the part it has so far. This is because these philanthropies want to see an impact and see "exactly how much you are moving the needle." It is clear that the collaborative, which in itself coordinates resources for community benefit, is in need of consistent and more significant philanthropy. It is important to note that while philanthropy has played such an essential role in helping to launch and support community partnerships, philanthropic resources are not guaranteed and often not long term. How to sustain community partnerships is an ongoing concern, as these formations are engaged in such vital activities, yet they are not always sustained over time. Keeping partnerships going and conducting relevant work is actually work in itself. For some community partnerships, attaining adequate ongoing funding is the most challenging effort of all.

The SELA Collaborative is an important type of community partnership that both coordinates resources across organizations that are assets to the community and focuses its work on enhancing the civic engagement and organizational capacity of community residents. This is not a partnership that connects residents to jobs among the local large employers, as in the case of community partnerships built around anchor institutions such as universities or hospitals. The SELA Collaborative focuses on a different aspect of the ecosystem of organizations in its region.

## NOTES

1. http://selacollab.org/aboutus/.
2. http://selacollab.org/aboutus/.
3. https://upswell.org/2018/10/03/southeast-los-angeles-collaborative-community -tour-empowering-sela-residents/.
4. http://selacollab.org/aboutus/.
5. http://selacollab.org/wp-content/uploads/2020/04/SELA_Collab_Case_Study -Final-WEB-012820.pdf.

# 8. Central Corridor Anchor Partnership

The Central Corridor Anchor Partnership (CCAP) was established in 2012 as a way in which anchor institutions within the Minnesota-St. Paul region could work together to support the twin cities. CCAP is a group of colleges, universities, hospitals, and health-care organizations located near the Green Line in Minneapolis-St. Paul. Current hospitals and college CCAP members are Augsburg University, Fairview Health Services, Hennepin Healthcare, Metropolitan State University, Minneapolis Community and Technical College, Regions Hospital/HealthPartners, St. Catherine University, Saint Paul College, and the University of St. Thomas. Additionally, U.S. Bank and Wells Fargo are members of the partnership.

The partnership seeks to maximize the role that anchor institutions play within their own community, in order to benefit the anchors themselves as well as the local region. CCAP focuses on three main aspects of anchor-driven investment in the local community: workforce development, increasing local procurement, and public transportation growth and development.

CCAP was conceived in 2010 by the McKnight Foundation and the Central Corridor Funders Collaborative. After a 2011 Living Cities meeting, the idea for an anchor institution partnership came to life, and the partnership was formally established in 2012. Initial financial support for the creation of the partnership was provided by the McKnight Foundation and the Central Corridor Funders Collaborative. The creation of the partnership was also supported by prominent local figures within the 'eds and meds' – these figures became initial Corridors of Opportunity partners.

## GEOGRAPHICAL, HISTORICAL, AND CULTURAL CONTEXT

The Central Corridor, as used by the CCAP, refers to neighborhoods surrounding the METRO Green Line, an 11 mile light-rail transit line connecting Minneapolis and St. Paul, Minnesota. The line links five major centers of activity in the twin cities region: downtown Minneapolis, the University of Minnesota, the Midway area, the State Capitol complex, and downtown St. Paul. Before opening in June 2014, the line was referred to as the Central Corridor LRT (light-rail transit).

In the 1990s, the Minneapolis-St. Paul region was 79% white, with sub-urban residential job growth outpacing the central cities, which increasingly developed larger concentrations of poverty. As the nation reeled from spikes in violent crime during the 1990s, so did Minneapolis. In 1995, the city's crime rate was higher than New York City's, dubbing the city "Murderapolis."

With crime hindering economic development in the city's south side, employers, foundations, government, and nonprofits used job training con-nected to positions in the nearby hospital, redevelopment of housing, new infrastructure, and new community-driven tactics to reduce crime.

Regional trends began to undermine progress for inner-city neighborhoods and residents. Suburban sprawl shifted public resources from city centers to expand highways and sewers into the far reaches of the region, increasingly isolating low-income city residents from the new jobs and housing that fol-lowed, especially in the absence of a robust regional transportation system.

In 2013, the Central Corridor region had a population of 107,000 – an increase of 14% from a decade earlier. The region was 56% white, 24% black, and 13% Asian. Income in the Central Corridor lagged behind the overall Minnesota-St. Paul average, at $41,500 compared to $49,757.

## STRATEGY

The partnership's main goal is to secure regional prosperity in the Minnesota-St. Paul region, while creating wealth in communities adjacent to the Central Corridor. CCAP aims to accomplish this by focusing and aggregating demand from the Anchor institutions to local suppliers that employ and invest in the community. This strategy speaks to the interdependence across an ecosystem of institutions in a region. Their strategy emphasizes both regional pros-perity as well as the economic well-being of residents in immediately local communities.

CCAP exists due to the investments of the Central Corridor Funders Collaborative and the McKnight Foundation, as well as the efforts of two local development experts: Louis Smith, a Minneapolis attorney whose work with South Minneapolis's Phillips Partnership helped to spur the resurgence of the Midtown Greenway/Lake Street corridor; and Ellen Watters, a civic source principal whose lengthy resume includes stints as president of the Midway Chamber of Commerce and vice president of economic development for the St. Paul Chamber of Commerce. Here is another example of private philanthropy's role, particularly in helping to launch the partnership. Local philanthropy is positioned to provide the capital to help bring partners together and engage experts at the outset.

Key aspects of the partnership's mission involve increasing investment in Central Corridor businesses, hiring more residents from Central Corridor neighborhoods, and increasing transit use by students and employees. Moreover, the partnership seeks to augment the quality of physical infrastructure in the region that serves patients, students, and employees. All of the partnership's principles and goals maintain an essential focus on the health, vitality, and growth of surrounding neighborhoods.

Anchor partners participating in CCAP commit to investing in local physical infrastructure serving members of the Central Corridor community. CCAP uses the term "anchor" to indicate the important role each partner plays in the Central Corridor economy and to describe how each partner is anchored to the growth and success of surrounding neighborhoods. Each anchor partner has committed its chief executive officer or authorized senior executive representative to participate in quarterly partnership meetings to provide policy guidance and strategic direction; senior staff participation in work groups to shape and implement our initiatives; and financial support. CCAP anchor partner capacity comprises 19 zip codes, 60,000 employees, and 112,000 students. The anchor institutions have a combined $2.5 billion in annual spending.

## FUNDING THE WORK

The partnership was conceived and supported in its earliest stages by two key local philanthropies. One of these is the McKnight Foundation, a Minneapolis-based philanthropy whose grants support regional economic and community development, Minnesota's arts and artists, education equity, and youth engagement, among other focus areas.

The Central Corridor Funders Collaborative was the other key philanthropy involved in the founding of the CCAP. This, which closed formally in 2016, was a partnership among 14 local foundations to ensure that the Green Line light rail project brought tangible benefits to neighborhoods along its route. The collaborative was given an intentionally limited lifespan and an extremely focused goal – a 10-year window to intervene in a massive public infrastructure investment to help ensure that low-income people and neighborhoods along the Green Line benefit from the investment.

## PROGRAM OVERVIEW

### Workforce

The key goal for CCAP's workforce initiatives is to secure regional prosperity directly through hiring Central Corridor residents. It also aims to achieve a workforce among anchor institutions that is more representative of local communities along the Central Corridor. By doing this, CCAP seeks to contribute towards better local health outcomes, improved educational attainment, and increased household incomes. CCAP established three key objectives in pursuit of this goal:

1.  Increase anchor institution employment from central corridor zip codes from 13% to 18% in five years. (CCAP has already met its initial goal of hiring more local residents at member institutions: 19% of employees now live in Central Corridor neighborhoods.)
2.  Achieve racial diversity goals across all job categories among Central Corridor anchor institutions in five years.
3.  Reduce the racial employment gap in the Central Corridor zip codes from 14% to 10% in five years.

Many of these jobs are in the fast-growing health-care field. This momentum is expected to continue as more young people entering the job market have participated in CCAP-sponsored programs such as Scrubs Camp, which gives high school students a taste of college life studying health sciences, and Central Corridor College (C3 Fellows) Fellowship program, which provides inner-city students on two- and four-year college courses paid work in health-care fields while still in school.

## Procurement

CCAP's procurement goal is to create wealth in communities adjacent to the Central Corridor by focusing and aggregating the demand from the Anchor institutions to local suppliers that employ and invest in the community. This procurement strategy focuses on increasing the amount of local purchasing made by anchor institutions by 5% over 2012 data, as well as creating cost savings over time for anchors through collective procurement. Three main strategies are followed in pursuit of these objectives: driving anchor purchasing to local vendors and tracking results; developing below list pricing or joint contracts for local suppliers; and growing or attracting suppliers to the corridor to meet out-of-state anchor spend.

Some of the partner institutions have successfully redirected resources to a local supply chain. Augsburg University, for example, spent 15% of funds devoted to a new science center on local-, minority-, or female-owned businesses, amounting to more than $9 million. Additionally, HealthEast Healthcare System now serves 8,000 pounds of locally grown vegetables in its kitchens each year.

**Transit**

CCAP also aims to provide a convenient, affordable range of transportation options to local residents, employees, and students in the Central Corridor. It seeks to ensure the full utilization of the Green Line and other transit to connect to economic opportunities. Key objectives include increasing transit use among anchors by 5% in five years and improving last-mile connections to the Green Line via bus, biking, and walking.

Employees and students at anchor institutions can now ride light rail or buses for less, thanks to a CCAP program in which anchors offer discounted transit cards. At Minneapolis College, transit use jumped 30% after the introduction of the program.

## PROGRAMMING AGENDA AND IMPACT

CCAP uses data collection to assess progress on initiatives throughout the region. It pursues data that are qualified by race, among other factors. New strategies and initiatives are continually introduced, closed, and examined through yearly reports that detail whether progress has been made towards achieving CCAP's key goals. Goals are often expanded as progress is made, hence there is continual, unceasing progress being driven towards securing regional prosperity for neighborhoods in the Central Corridor.

CCAP has worked to identify a local employment gap in terms of health-care employees and workplace accessibility. CCAP set a goal for the percentage of employees that reside in zip codes surrounding their place of employment, and have met that goal. CCAP has also conducted research analyzing poverty and income data in the census tracts along the Corridor, and has been credited with contributing to how investment in the Corridor's light rail has boosted incomes and reduced poverty.

## NONPROFITS AND PHILANTHROPY

CCAP activities are funded by philanthropic contributions. The partnership's philosophy envisions how infrastructure investment could leverage gains in equity and economic opportunity in the region. CCAP considers philanthropy's role as "rocket fuel"[1] for the design of employment and workforce initiatives, but necessitates that philanthropy proves its value to employers and colleges in the region. Over time, CCAP's goal is to reduce foundation funding and increase reliance on health-care employers which value CCAP as a recruiting source for local, talented employees.

CCAP works with numerous nonprofits as workforce development partners, and relies on their ability to provide strong "wrap-around" services that support burdened college students who are the main target of workforce initiatives. Nonprofits are CCAP's partners in designing workforce initiatives, and they support these programs as well.

## LESSONS AND DIRECTIONS

CCAP has been largely successful, but it still faces challenges in certain areas that it has struggled to overcome. For instance, CCAP's C3 Fellows program supports the development of students towards entry-level health-care jobs. However, too few entry-level positions are available. This is a structural problem, as deeply entrenched protocols prevent health-care institutions from billing for work performed by noncredentialed employees, including the students that C3 Fellows serves.

In coming years, CCAP intends to maintain focus on the pursuit of its key goals surrounding transport, procurement, and workforce development. It plans to expand programs and initiatives, such as the C3 Fellows program, to reach a greater number of students. The development of programs that provide formal degrees and certificates is also in progress, due to increasing demand from employers for these qualifications.

This is another community partnership that is leveraging anchor institutions to channel their resources toward community benefit. This is clearly an important trend in community partnerships in the U.S. CCAP has been engaging local anchor institutions in using their employment opportunities and purchasing power to close longstanding gaps in their locality and region. While some of the partners are corporations, most of them are larger nonprofit organizations. This is also another example of a community partnership that has leveraged philanthropy to launch its work.

## COVID-19 RESPONSE

In the COVID-19 pandemic, CCAP has been coordinating its health-care partners in response to workforce changes. Initially, the pandemic caused many layoffs and furloughs in the health-care field. But as the situation continued, workforce needs increased. Through the C3 Fellows program, CCAP has been working to mobilize, support, and train students who have a long-term interest in building health-care careers. CCAP provides support, mentoring, and coaching throughout their fellowships. One main focal point from this program has been the tension between a student's schedule and a hospital shift, which has prompted CCAP to promote ideas about best practices for flexibility with student employment experiences in health care.

Indeed, the pandemic highlighted the significance of health care and careers in the field. As CCAP had already convened health institutions through its collaboration and programming, it was able to leverage its existing C3 Fellows program to continue developing a pipeline for a future health-care workforce. As the pandemic has expanded interest in health careers in general, CCAP was able to apply its existing efforts to begin meeting increased interest as well as increased needs from health institutions.

## NOTE

1.   L. Smith (counsel for CCAP), personal communication, February 1, 2021.

# 9. Quality Jobs Fund

The Quality Jobs Fund (QJF) offers an alternative model of community partnership. This is an initiative involving financing to intermediary organizations in order to expand access to stable, well-paying jobs with benefits for historically underserved populations. Each intermediary, in effect, collaborates not only with partners in their locality, but also with a national foundation and a bank in California. The Central Valley Fund Capital Partners (CVF) is an example of an intermediary that has received an investment from the QJF. It operates locally, investing in small businesses in its region.

## BACKGROUND OF THE PARTNERSHIP

The Federal Home Loan Bank of San Francisco and the New World Foundation (NWF) launched the QJF based on an extensive research and planning process in 2017. The Federal Home Loan Bank of San Francisco was chartered by Congress to help local lenders invest in jobs, housing, and economic growth in local communities. The bank has historically worked through local government partnerships with initiatives and community organizations to attract more investment and resources to expand economic development opportunities in communities. The NWF is a philanthropic nonprofit organization in New York which aims to support organizations that aid communities, advance democracy, and protect civil rights. The NWF operates as a national community foundation (public charity) that houses numerous funds with particular themes and intentions. QJF is a $100 million donor-advised fund[1] housed at NWF intended to support the development of underserved working-class communities through quality job expansion, mainly in California, Arizona, and Nevada. The fund aims to seed sustainable and well-paid jobs and skill upgrading for working individuals. The overarching goal is to address issues of inequality through such quality job growth and skill development for a diverse workforce.[2]

The strategy behind QJF was developed through collaboration with the Aspen Institute, a nonprofit think tank, on an intensive study and planning process that involved roundtable meetings with community leaders, business leaders, labor leaders, academics, job training professionals, and national and regional experts. The comprehensive planning process focused on developing

59

the QJF initiative to help tackle the issue of closing the wealth gap by address-ing some barriers preventing the upward mobility of working-class families.[3]

The bank and NWF intend for QJF investments to support innovative initiatives by organizations that provide debt or equity financing to small businesses in order to aid business growth and create sustainable, long-term, well-paid jobs in underserved communities. Organizations that are candidates for QJF investment must have a track record of preparing individuals for higher-paying, quality jobs through training and upskilling. They must qualify as an intermediary, meaning they must provide expansion capital to under-served areas of the small business market. In creating middle-class jobs, the initiative ultimately aims to enable more working families to be able to afford to buy homes and help build strong communities.

In 2018, QJF invested $5 million in CVF to support quality job creation and small businesses in California's Central Valley region. This was the first investment made by QJF. CVF, based in Davis, California, is a private equity firm established in 2005 to finance economic growth through investments in lower middle-market businesses. Managing over $350 million in committed capital since 2005, CVF focuses on investing mainly in California and through-out the western U.S. CVF offers flexible capital solutions and the network and expertise to help businesses thrive. CVF usually provides mezzanine capital[4] through subordinated debt[5] and preferred stock investments.[6]

QJF forms a unique collaboration between the Federal Home Loan Bank of San Francisco, NWF, and CVF. CVF invests in businesses in the western U.S., particularly in underserved areas such as California's Central Valley region. It remains the financial partner of choice for Central Valley small and medium-sized business owners. CVF makes long-term investments in interme-diaries which serve particular localities within the valley. In this way, CVF can use the investment from QJF to help businesses that reach specific underserved communities in the area through quality job building and business expansion.

QJF investments focus on increasing wages for working families, and thus increasing the pool of potential homebuyers and helping sustain vibrant communities. Such goals attract attention and support from local governments. FHLBank San Francisco's presence in the partnership bolsters local govern-ments' belief that QJF investments can lead to more investment and resources coming into local communities, thereby expanding economic development opportunities. The positions of the bank and NWF have the ability to leverage CVF's capacity to collaborate with local government, local business, and the local economy. Stockton, California mayor Michael Tubbs said that QJF can provide essential access to capital for small businesses; the investments can strengthen communities.[7] QJF therefore has the ability to expand the capacity of existing community partnerships like CVF. The QJF investment gives CVF additional visibility and can strengthen its relationship with local government.

Consequently, funding from beyond CVF's locality has helped enhance its ability to enter into cross-sector community partnerships with other entities, including local government. This external funding through QJF actually facilitates and strengthens community partnerships in this instance.

## GEOGRAPHICAL, HISTORICAL, AND CULTURAL CONTEXT

California's Central Valley extends from Shasta County in the north to Kern County in the south, and covers about 18,000 square miles. The area is surrounded by several mountain ranges and includes Sacramento Valley and San Joaquin Valley. Population centers in the valley include Redding, Sacramento, Stockton, Porterville, Modesto, Fresno, and Bakersfield. About 7 million people live in the valley, considered the fastest growing region in the state.

The Central Valley is recognized as an area of rich farmland important for the region's local economy and for U.S. agricultural production. Notably, Sacramento's economy has made headway in expanding and diversifying its economy, following nearby hubs like the San Francisco Bay Area. The population in the area has grown as persons from the San Francisco Bay Area seek lower housing costs. Immigration has also boomed in the area, with populations coming from Asia, Central America, Mexico, and Eastern Europe.[8]

There are numerous historically undercounted demographic groups in the Central Valley, including non-U.S. citizens, African Americans, Native Americans, and Latinx Americans. Examining eight cities in this region – Woodland, Stockton, Modesto, Merced, Fresno, Hanford, Visalia, and Bakersfield – 40–50% of the population was Hispanic/Latino in 2017. Latino incomes equate to 84% of the incomes for all households in these communities. In 2017, the median household incomes of these cities ranged from less than $43,000 per year (Fresno) to over $59,000 (Bakersfield); the median household income for the entire state of California was over $66,000 per year.[9] However, the per capita income of valley counties has fallen further behind the state average over the years. The population, though, has accounted for a steadily rising share of the state population, especially between 1975 and 2010 as residents sought lower housing prices and less urban living. In 1975, the valley had 8.3% of the state population; in 2010, 10.7%; in 2018, 10.8%.[10]

As the price of living in many of California's coastal areas has become more costly over the years, more and more people have been priced out of residential housing; in 2017, California's median home value was up 66% from its low in 2012.[11] As of 2019, the median price for a house in California topped $600,000, more than twice the national level.[12] In October 2020, the median sold price of existing single-family homes was $1,100,999 in the San Francisco Bay Area but $395,000 in the valley.[13] Thus, Californians have moved to more affordable areas in the state such as the Central Valley region. Many of these people still retain employment in cities outside the valley and must commute to their area of employment.

The Central Valley region is a historically underserved region. Particular areas like the San Joaquin Valley lag behind the rest of California in many social and economic measures, including unemployment levels and poverty rate. The Central Valley counties have persistently performed poorly compared to state averages on key economic indicators such as per capita income, unemployment, and poverty rates.[14] Average educational attainment in these counties is also well below the state average.[15] The U.S. Bureau of Labor Statistics reported six of the ten highest metropolitan unemployment rates in the country to be found in the valley for March 2020. One major issue in the valley is also its major industry – agriculture. The valley has been largely unable to diversify its mostly rural economic base, highlighting the region's vulnerability in the face of recession. Moreover, faced with new policies to increase the sustainability of groundwater management in agricultural production, the region may be faced with new economic pressures and challenges due to economic dependency on mostly agriculture.

Another barrier to economic development in the valley has been issues with workforce. With the reputation as an underserved region – San Joaquin Valley has even been referred to as the "Appalachia of the West" and the "Valley of the Poor" – some community leaders believe the region has been burdened with a sense of hopelessness that can discourage bold economic thinking. The valley has been faced with issues such as the inability to diversify its largely rural economic base.[16]

In most valley counties, graduation rates are lower than the state average. But the founding of UC Merced in 2005 has contributed to the educational and economic growth of the region. UC Merced strives to help improve the standard of education within the valley through educational outreach centers in Bakersfield and Fresno which offer professional development programs, high school programs, and other opportunities for students. UC Merced is one of the largest employers in Merced County with more than 1,500 employees. The campus's economic contribution to the region and to California has been more than $23 billion since the beginning of operations in 2000.[17] There are still issues with closing the educational gap between other areas, ultimately maintaining the challenge of building a more modern and diverse economy in the valley.

## STRATEGY

QJF is a collaborative project of the NWF and the Federal Home Loan Bank of San Francisco to address some of the problems of local economic decline and resulting inequality through advancing economic opportunity and building community. Through a $100 million investment in quality job creation, QJF aims to enhance community wealth and the potential of working families by seeding sustainable long-term community well-being programs in distressed communities of Arizona, California, and Nevada. The core of QJF funding is in the form of investments – forgivable loans based on performance in agreements. The goal is to address problems of inequality through quality job expansion and skill development. Through long-term investments in intermediaries that serve particular localities, QJF uses a series of community partnerships to achieve its goal.

The initiative is formed around the idea that community stakeholders drive progress. Rising long-term underdevelopment and decline in homeownership negatively impacts people's lives locally and nationally. QJF aims to support the development of strong and sustainable working-class communities through the provision of well-paid jobs and skill-upgrading programs for workers. QJF investments focus on helping to increase wages for working families, thereby increasing the pool of potential homebuyers and helping sustain vibrant communities.

QJF investments have been distributed over the course of several years beginning in 2017. Qualifying intermediaries are required to meet the criteria for innovative new programs, or to have a proven track record of providing debt or equity financing to small businesses to support business expansion and job creation and preparing individuals for higher-paying, quality jobs through job training and upskilling. Some QJF investments will be recycled on a continuous basis for reinvestment.

Through the Federal Home Loan Bank of San Francisco and the NWF, the QJF awards funds to qualifying intermediaries such as the Central Valley Fund for its economic development initiatives.

CVF invests in small and medium-sized businesses that serve particular communities in the valley. CVF works with business owners to develop a capital structure that best fits their personal and business needs. After closing an investment, CVF provides its portfolio companies with significant personal attention, unique in the marketplace. CVF has experience in several important markets on the West Coast, and maintains a strong local presence in the valley, with offices in Davis and Fresno. Additionally, CVF has deep knowledge of the Hispanic market with relationships with Hispanic business owners and investors throughout the U.S. and Mexico. CVF has made several investments in the Pacific northwest and has developed a network of entrepreneurs, banks, and intermediaries in the region.[18]

# PROGRAM OVERVIEW

### Eligibility for Quality Jobs Fund Direct Investment

Organizations seeking funds from QJF must qualify as an intermediary. An intermediary is an entity that acts to support the provision of services by another entity rather than providing direct services itself. Intermediaries tend to connect smaller organizations and the people they serve to the local delivery system.[19] Organizations and intermediaries include investment funds, nonprofits, and social impact venture funds focused on skill upgrading and business-focused economic development to receive investments to expand existing operations or create new programs. Intermediaries are chosen based on innovative new programs and longstanding ventures with a proven track record in either (a) providing expansion capital to underserved segments of the small business market or (b) successfully implementing skill development and training programs that result in higher-quality jobs.[20] Intermediaries can play distinct roles within an ecosystem of organizations in communities. They are neither large employers nor grassroots nonprofits. They are positioned to operate in-between and across numerous different types of organizations in different fields and of varying sizes.

### Evaluation Criteria for Quality Jobs Fund Direct Investment

Prospects for QJF financing are evaluated based on numerous criteria, which vary depending on the mission of the intermediary, but include many of the below categories:[21]

1. Capability – defined as experience and business structure; what is needed to build a tailored portfolio to address cross-cutting insights and intervene where skill-building and capital access gaps exist.
2. Track record of improving wages of lower-income workers.
3. Ability to leverage a QJF investment to harness additional resources.
4. Minimum asset base and minimum track record in middle-skilled job sector.
5. Demonstrated linkages with employers in the region.
6. Senior staff experience and capacity.
7. Experience incorporating policy, training, and technical assistance into programs.
8. Commitment to recruiting and training women and minorities.
9. Track record of investing in businesses that increase quality jobs.
10. Track record of providing capital to small, medium-sized, minority-owned, or employee-owned businesses.

**Quality Jobs Fund Operations**

In the QJF partnership, NWF is responsible for surveying the field, conducting due diligence for grantmaking purposes, and spearheading, monitoring, and evaluating the grant investments that are made. NWF also evaluates inquiries about QJF and manages invitations to applicants for the selection process.

# PROGRAMMING AGENDA AND DIRECTIONS

CVF has been using the invested $5 million from QJF in 2018 to support businesses in the Central Valley region, which includes flexible capital to companies like Initiative Foods, an organic baby food manufacturer in Sanger, California, to help create and sustain quality jobs. Using $5 million in debt and equity financing from the CVF to buy new factory equipment, Initiative Foods' expansion will lead to 30 more jobs that, because of the high-tech status of the equipment, will pay much more than past positions in the company. At the same time, the company has been working to increase the hourly wage of employees. CVF also gave $8.75 million to Utility Telecom in Stockton to help expand business operations and grow and offer quality jobs.[22]

QJF demonstrates creative leveraging of private-sector tactics for social ends through its unique partnership between a cooperative bank and a foundation with an established background in community and economic equity. It also harnesses active engagement from local governments. The NWF has contracted with Marga Incorporated to embark on a learning agenda in order to understand the unique qualities and impacts of QJF. While QJF is a focused initiative, investing in 12 intermediary organizations, each working on projects specific to their local communities, the idea of QJF is to inform broader ideas (and perhaps policies ultimately) that alter approaches to employment.

With the emergence of a gig economy and declines in unionization (particularly in the U.S.), stable jobs with benefits have been on the decline for decades. The implications for local communities have been significant. The increased wealth gap has been very significant, and exacerbated by the COVID-19 pandemic. With more widespread jobs with greater stability and higher incomes, underserved populations will have greater purchasing power to enable increases in homeownership, greater access to education, and improved health. It QJF is successful over the coming years, it will provide important lessons that can inform how to support higher-quality employment and close dramatic wealth and income gaps.

In the long term, QJF can attract more investment and resources to communities, particularly in the western U.S., expanding economic development opportunities in communities. QJF can provide critical access to capital for small businesses to create jobs and can provide investments that strengthen the community, increase the pool of potential homebuyers, and fortify the financial security of working families in the short term and future. The multifaceted learning agenda underway should provide informative insights, as it is assessing the impact of QJF investments on intermediaries, businesses, employees, and communities.

## COVID-19 RESPONSE

As QJF is a relatively new program, intermediaries were early in the process of establishing necessary partnerships in their communities to lead to quality jobs. Some had received an initial tranche of investment just months before the arrival of the COVID-19 pandemic. In response to the pandemic, NWF contacted all QJF investees, including CVF, in order to learn how the pandemic was affecting the investees' communities and work. NWF then communicated these challenges to the bank in order to inform changes to QJF. With the bank's approval, NWF even created new pools of funding for grants to supplement the intermediaries' work, which was significantly disrupted by the pandemic.

The CVF team created a Coronavirus Scorecard in response to the pandemic in order to highlight the business status, liquidity, indebtedness, and action steps ahead for each CVF company. CVF is also adapting its portfolio with numerous recommendations and decisions. Working individually with each company, it is helping to implement actions such as deferring interest payments and sales tax, rent, and utility bills. CVF is working with the companies to explore opportunities for rapid-response supply chain diversification.

CVF encouraged companies to file for relief through the U.S. Small Business Administration's Paycheck Protection Program. This program provides businesses resources primarily to help companies maintain their payroll and keep their workers employed. Every CVF company has been legally classified as an "essential business," in accordance with respective state definitions. This classification is helpful in filing for relief and seeking forgiveness in the future if money was solely used to keep workers or rehire positions cut due to the pandemic. CVF has also created a customized dossier for each company that might be eligible for relief so that they can track money spent that could meet forgiveness criteria.

The CVF team predicts numerous challenges for its companies due to fallout from the COVID-19 pandemic. There are major delays in filing for relief because of delays in lender operations. Big bank lenders have also been inundated by relief applications, and in many cases, the banks have prioritized their best customers. Such practices not only contribute to filing delays but also impact the numbers that will be left out in underserved and rural markets. Community banks, however, have been largely more successful in processing applications.

CVF has offered expertise to business owners on how to keep business afloat during the coronavirus pandemic through live webinars and other support. Brad Triebsch, a managing partnership with CVF, suggests that business leaders should explore different markets than their usual operations and work within something that is now more relevant during the pandemic, if they can. Operators should consider asking vendors and landlords for extended terms or forbearance on payment, and for banks to be accommodating with potential loan modifications or interest-only payments. Triebsch also suggests to draft a narrative as soon as possible on how the business has been reacting to the downturn; keeping records, emails, and payment records can be used to illustrate why money was needed and how it was spent, in order to avoid issues in the future.

Overall, QJF, through local intermediaries such as CVF, provides a compelling model of a community partnership which creatively leverages funding from a bank to drive a clearly nonprofit strategy. As a nonprofit and a philanthropic institution with a social and economic justice mission, the NWF became an ideal destination for the bank's funding. QJF depends on the combination of funding from private industry and the perspective and experience of NWF. This is a clear example of a partnership that benefits greatly from the active engagement of nonprofits and philanthropy. The transactional nature of financing in banking, complemented by the approach of a nonprofit and philanthropic entity such as NWF, is an important combination. NWF's history of grantmaking in communities across the U.S. and assessing community-based initiatives' potential to influence social and economic change is a dimension that enables a lens of understanding that helps identify prospective investees and assess their progress.

Community partnerships in the U.S. take varying forms, as demonstrated in these five examples. Because of the presence of a robust nonprofit sector, community partnerships in the U.S. are particularly dynamic. These partnerships involve nonprofits and philanthropic institutions of all types. They all have in common some form of a social mission. They exist to solve a problem or a series of problems in their localities or regions. Strategic thinking is fundamental in determining how these partnerships are structured and programmatically designed. They must identify appropriate partners and organize collaborative models that make use of their respective assets in some mutually beneficial fashion. They are also challenged to develop programming that can actually begin to solve the problems that led to the partners coming together.

The perspective of nonprofit organizations situates these community partnerships to pursue a common good in their localities or regions. These partnerships are not designed for the sole benefit of the participating organizations. They are driven by a higher mission to solve problems in a locality. They transcend self-advocacy or transactional projects for profit. Many of these partnerships are nonprofit-like in their orientation, and some of them are actual nonprofit organizations. They are new forms of governance, but not, in any way, governmental substitutes. But they are civil society formations that both fill gaps that government has not filled and enable strategic analysis that transcends government. Their thinking is not limited by existing governmental structures. But they can effectively collaborate with government. Some of these partnerships align their intentions with local government. This is probably wise given the consistency and stability of government, but it is not foolproof due to the fluidity of changes in governmental administrations. This inconsistent aspect of government actually speaks to the significance of community partnerships. Community partnerships can become consistent civil society formations that raise expectations of what is possible in a locality in areas such as employment and health. Particularly when they include anchor institutions, they are positioned to create a different kind of stability.

In a democracy such as the U.S., everyone has a role in continuously improving society. In many ways, this role starts at home – at the local level. There is a need for a healthy and robust and responsive government at all levels – in the U.S. case – federal, state, and local. Ideally, government should ensure to the highest possible degree the health and well-being of the population. Striving for effective governments is a continuous process. But civil society also has a role to play. Community partnerships provide a wide variety of ways in which this civic responsibility can be manifested. The role of nonprofits and philanthropy in forging, maintaining, and strengthening these community partnerships is indispensable. We are only beginning to see the potential of community partnerships as agents of change in the U.S.

## NOTES

1.  A donor-advised fund is a giving vehicle created at a public charity which allows donors to make charitable contributions, receive an immediate tax deduction, and then recommend grants from the fund over time (www.nptrust.org/what-is-a-donor-advised-fund/).
2.  http://qualityjobsfund.org/the-fund/.
3.  https://newwf.org/100-million-investment-quality-job-creation/.
4.  Mezzanine capital is a form of financing that is part debt and part equity. It incorporates equity-based options with a lower-priority debt to provide flexible long-term capital for use in buy-outs or growth financing (www.attractcapital.com/mezzanine-capital.html).
5.  Subordinated debt generally refers to debt securities that have a secondary or lesser claim to the issuer's assets than more senior debt (https://financial-dictionary.thefreedictionary.com/Subordinated+debt).
6.  Preferred stocks are a type of investment that pays interest or dividends to investors before dividends are paid to common stockholders.

7. https://cvfcapitalpartners.com/blog/press-releases/central-valley-fund-announced -as-first-investment-of-the-%24100-million-quality-jobs-fund/.
8. www.ppic.org/content/pubs/jtf/JTF_CentralValleyJTF.pdf.
9. www.edhovee.com/edhblog/2018/7/25/californias-central-valley-guideposts-to -success.
10. www.ccsce.com/PDF/Numbers-May2019-Central-Valley-Economic-and -Demographic-Trends.pdf.
11. www.ppic.org/wp-content/uploads/r-118hjr.pdf.
12. www.bloomberg.com/graphics/2019-california-housing-crisis/.
13. www.noradarealestate.com/blog/california-housing-market/.
14. www.ccsce.com/PDF/Numbers-May2019-Central-Valley-Economic-and -Demographic-Trends.pdf.
15. The valley accounts for 9.7% of the state population over 18 but also accounts for 14.9% of residents who did not go to high school and only 4.4% of state residents with a graduate degree.
16. www.sacbee.com/news/california/big-valley/article233551287.html.
17. www.ucmerced.edu/about.
18. https://cvfcapitalpartners.com/about/cvf-capital-partners/.
19. https://link.springer.com/referenceworkentry/10.1007%2F978-0-387-93996 -4_46.
20. http://qualityjobsfund.org/get-involved/.
21. http://qualityjobsfund.org/a-100-million-investment-in-quality-job-creation/
22. https://newwf.org/100-million-investment-quality-job-creation/.

# PART III

# International community partnerships

# 10. Introduction to Part III

While community partnerships involving large local nonprofit employers starting with the assistance of private philanthropy have been characteristic of many emerging community partnerships in the U.S., many international contexts do not have substantial nonprofit and philanthropic sectors. Of course, this varies significantly depending on the country and local context. Part III is based on an extensive search for examples of community partnerships in different parts of the world with an intent to represent multiple continents – South America, Africa, Europe, Asia, and Australia.

These partnerships are extremely varied but still remain consistent with the theme of community partnerships that include organizations representing different fields or sectors, and include some involvement of nonprofit organizations and philanthropy.

# 11. Colombia: Rebuilding El Salado

Rebuilding El Salado is a peace-building partnership between armed conflict victims from El Salado, Semana Foundation (SF), and other stakeholders that aim to overcome tragic consequences in this rural territory. Colombia has endured the longest-running armed conflict in the Western Hemisphere. More than 60 years of confrontation among guerrilla, government, and paramilitary forces have caused enormous loss of life and weakened the rule of law.[1] Multiple efforts, such as the demobilization of paramilitary forces in 2005 and the peace agreement between the Revolutionary Armed Forces of Columbia (FARC) and the government in 2016, have aimed to end the armed conflict in Colombia. Nevertheless, peace remains unattainable. Inequality, the lack of effective agrarian reforms, weak state capability, corruption, and disputes to gain a monopoly over the illicit drug market may explain the origin of the conflict and the reasons why it is still ongoing.

Colombia's armed conflict has caused 262,000 deaths, 80,472 enforced disappearances, 15,738 victims of sexual violence, and 7.7 million victims of forced displacement.[2] One of the most afflicted areas is Montes de María, located on the northern coast of Colombia. Montes de María is an agricultural subregion consisting of 15 municipalities. Since 1970, crossfire between guerrilla groups, paramilitary forces, and the army has taken place in this territory.[3] About 60 massacres were committed and 200,000 people fled their homes to urban areas escaping from violence.[4]

El Salado is one of the rural territories of Montes de María. This municipality not only suffered from the violence of armed conflict, it has also not received sufficient reparation support from the government, leaving many to feel abandoned by authorities. With the support of organizations from the public, private, and philanthropic sectors, a community partnership transformed the scenario of violence to peace and opportunity. It was established by Claudia Garcia, director of SF: "years ago, more than 400 paramilitaries took to the streets of El Salado and carried out 60 massacres throughout the area. Today, those same streets and those same mountains are flooded with future."

## EL SALADO MASSACRE

El Salado is a small town located in Carmen de Bolívar, Montes de María. It was one of the most prosperous areas of the region, due to the manufacturing of tobacco. El Salado is also known for its cattle breeding, the production of agricultural products like manioc and corn, and exports of tobacco and other products, which allowed the community to cover their basic needs. As with several territories in Montes de María, El Salado became a battlefield between different armed groups who spread terror to take control over the territory and the population. Due to the violence in the region, tobacco companies decided to abandon the area affecting the people and El Salado's economy.

On February 16, 2000, over 400 members of one of the most feared right-wing paramilitary groups (AUC) entered the town suspecting that the citizens were supporting their enemy, FARC (left-wing guerillas). Citizens were dragged to a local soccer field, where the paramilitaries publicly tortured and executed them. The massacre lasted six days and 60 people were murdered. Colombian marines observed the killings without doing anything to stop them.[5] This massive killing is thought to be one of the cruelest massacres by the paramilitaries. After the massacre, all the inhabitants fled their hometown and lived as displaced people in other cities of the country. Two years later, 120 *saladeros* decided to go back with the idea of rebuilding their homes and lives, without any assistance or protection from the government.

## SEMANA FOUNDATION

In April 2009, Semana, one of the most important media groups in Colombia, created SF[6] to develop post-conflict initiatives. The aim was to become active supporters of communities that were victims of the armed conflict.[7] The creation of SF took several months; the idea was discussed with social leaders, government officials, academia, the private sector, foundations, and nongovernmental organizations. The organization had many doubts on where to start and how to proceed: "how to support the economy of rural areas? where should we start to enable reparation of a victim? are we ready for the reintegration of ex-combatants into society?"[8]

Followed by a report made by a Semana journalist about the situation of El Salado eight years after the massacre, SF decided to pursue its first project: creating the first laboratory of peace in Colombia to rebuild El Salado and support the community. Given that this was the first project of SF and that initiatives of collective reparation in Colombia were almost nonexistent, SF did not have any preconceived procedures or mechanisms to intervene in the community. It had no plan or expertise in this matter.[9] The project was conceived as a collaborative initiative between the community, SF, and other partners.

## THE PROJECT: REBUILDING EL SALADO

The project Rebuilding El Salado lasted nine years. SF aimed to work in collaboration with the community and create state capability in that area. The project was unique and so successful that it was then replicated in other areas affected by the armed conflict in Colombia.

One of the most appealing traits of the partnership was the methodology implemented by SF. SF's team lived in El Salado, which allowed SF to build an authentic relationship with the community by comprehensively understanding its dynamics and needs. As Maria Alejandra Cabal, who used to work in El Salado, establishes, "if there was a roadblock everyone, including the team living there, will suffer from the roadblock."[10]

Additionally, SF and the community held several meetings to determine the action plan. During these meetings, the community expressed the needs of the municipality in terms of collective reparation and development. SF acted as a coordinator between the community and other organizations. Its role was to support the community to prioritize actions and link the needs and projects of El Salado with organizations that could collaborate. More than 100 partners from the public, private, and multilateral sectors worked along with the community.

In this instance, a foundation launched a community partnership with a particular purpose to rebuild a rural town. As a foundation, SF was started by a corporation. But it is not a longstanding, endowed, grantmaking institution like many foundations in the U.S. SF does, however, represent a version of philanthropy. This partnership was also created to fill a void left by local government. Over time, the partnership galvanized a significant number of organizations around the need to collectively overcome a devastating crisis.

## COMMUNITARIAN GOVERNANCE MODEL

To ensure accountability, transparency, effectiveness, and efficiency of the different initiatives, the community organized in different committees responsible for developing and supervising tasks, which allowed El Salado to develop a communitarian governance model. This governance model has also allowed the community to hold government accountable for providing services that were previously denied to them. It allowed the community to organize and monitor their actions as well as to understand how to effectively interact with other stakeholders. The following thematic committees were created to identify priorities and work with organizations and institutions present in the area.

1. *Committee on Infrastructure*: in charge of ensuring sustainability, effectiveness, and efficiency of the projects.

2. *Committee on Education and Culture*: in charge of advancing on projects related to improving the quality of education and fostering El Salado's culture among the inhabitants.
3. *Community Action Board*: the main governance organism in El Salado. Its members are in charge of all collective spaces in the area. The other committees are understood to be subordinated to the Community Action Board.
4. *Committee on Health*: in charge of advancing projects related to health care and manages the provision and commissioning of the Health Post before the Mayor's Office, the government, and other authorities.
5. *Action Board for Water-Related Issues*: in charge of providing drinking water to the population as well as preserving the solar panels that currently serve to provide water to the population.
6. *Committee on Economic Development*: in charge of monitoring and controlling productive projects in the region.

This model resulted in a comprehensive approach to solving a range of problems in El Salado. It speaks to the power of community partnerships. The collaboration among this blend of partners has created a new tool for addressing local concerns as well as holding government accountable.

## INITIATIVES

### Culture

The Caribbean Coast, where El Salado is located, is characterized by its unique cultural diversity. Before the massacre, the community of El Salado tended to gather at the House of Culture to tell stories about their region, sing, and dance. In February 2000, when the paramilitaries entered the town, they removed the instruments stored at the House of Culture. Then, they played them, while committing the massacre.

El Salado stopped gathering at the House of Culture for the 10 years following the massacre. Faced with the memory of horror and pain, the community also stopped celebrating their festivities with music. The *Saladeros* associated music with horror. The multiple initiatives developed in this project allowed the community to regain their culture and their common spaces. Two of the cultural projects developed are:

• *House of Culture*: rebuilding the House of Culture was established as a priority by the community because it represented a collective space. In partnership with the International Organization for Migration and Carvajal Foundation, Simon Hosie, a recognized architect of Colombia, worked along with the community to design a space that would accommodate their needs. He performed an ethnographic study to reflect the cultural and social heritage of El Salado. The House of Culture now has a library that is connected to the national library system, a place for meeting, and another one for social gatherings.

- *School of Music*: inaugurated in 2012. This is a space where children can learn how to play the traditional instruments of the region.

## Education

- *AEIOTÚ Kindergarten for children from 0 to 5 years old*: in partnership with government organizations and the Carulla Foundation,[11] the community created a center to welcome more than 120 children from El Salado and neighboring municipalities. This center is considered a high-quality space for children's development. Since its creation, studies have shown a 90% increase in the vocabulary of children and a 30% reduction in the difference between height and weight. In 2011, nonattendance to school was 42%, today it is 0%.
- *Secondary education*: before the massacre, the school lacked tenth and eleventh grades. In partnership with the secretary of education of Bolivar as well as SF, the community reopened the school and offered full secondary education. Furthermore, students can also access vocational studies – they can now graduate with a technical diploma in agriculture, which would allow them to contribute to the rural development of El Salado. To ensure the vocational studies of its youth, the community created a farm where students can meet the requirements to obtain their technical diploma in agriculture.

## Economic Development

In partnership with the Inter-American Development Bank (IDB) and other organizations, the community developed several initiatives to achieve comprehensive economic development. Some of the projects are the creation of the business of *hamadoras* (traditional furniture of El Salado), production of honey, and production of tobacco. It also partnered with one of the most important restaurants in Colombia to supply it with agricultural products.

## Infrastructure

- *Highways connecting El Salado with its neighbors*: El Salado did not have any paved roads. To travel to Carmen the Bolivar or other areas, it took people over eight hours. Now, with the paved roads, it only takes 15 minutes.

- *100 houses to the most vulnerable people*: in partnership with the government, the community gave 100 houses to the most vulnerable of El Salado. The community has also worked on ensuring adequate housing for every citizen of El Salado. Currently, 59% of the population owns a house.
- *Sewage*: in 2011, 93% of the population didn't have access to drinking water. Today, that same percentage of the population benefits from sewage and has access to drinking water.
- *House for the elders*: the elders created a space where they could meet and exchange their experiences.

## Health and Nutrition

- *Medical center*: in Montes de María, 93 of the 137 municipalities have medical centers. However, 52 of them don't have basic tools to operate and 64 of them don't have medical staff. El Salado had a health center that lacked medical staff and the necessary medical instruments. According to one of the *Saladeros*, "we had the center but there were no doctors, not even suture threads or needles."[12] In case of an emergency the community had to go to Carmen de Bolívar – over eight hours away in the absence of paved roads. Furthermore, only 25% of children had access to vaccines and 50% of them were undernourished. In partnership with the U.S. Agency for International Development, International Organization for Migration, and other foundations, the community now has a medical center, specializing in the most common sicknesses of people in El Salado.

## Security

- *Communication services*: one of the reasons why the massacre lasted for several days was because the community was not able to communicate with the authorities or the rest of Colombia. El Salado did not have mobile reception or access to Wi-Fi. Only 38% of the population had access to landline phones and 62% of the community lacked any means of communication. For this reason, the community prioritized access to communication services (cellphone and Wi-Fi) as a security matter. In partnership with Telefonica, the community now has access to Wi-Fi and mobile reception. Additionally, with the support of SF, the community now has a police station.

**Sports**

Soccer has become deeply ingrained in the Colombian identity and culture. At El Salado, soccer also represented an activity that united the community. In partnership with the President's Office, Pacific Rubiales, and SF, the community was able to build one of the most important soccer fields of the country. The community also created a school of soccer, in which everyone can participate. This initiative was led by youth.

## OTHER PROJECTS PERFORMED BY SEMANA FOUNDATION AND THE END OF OPERATIONS IN EL SALADO

The IDB contacted SF because it was interested in analyzing whether the methodology developed by SF in El Salado could be scalable to other areas in Colombia. Therefore, the IDB collaborated with SF to extend this methodology to Palenque and the Alta Montaña in Montes de Maria. Although the projects were different, the methodology of having a team living in the area and setting road maps with the community was developed in those areas.

SF continued working at El Salado and other areas across Colombia. In 2018, it ended its operations in El Salado. The initiative was never meant to last forever. Instead, the objective of SF was to build sustainable and effective state capability, enabling possibilities for the *saladeros* to successfully develop their own initiatives.

According to Maria Alejandra Cabal, in Colombia and in communities that have suffered from conflict, there's a lack of trust in government and a feeling that the governments owe things to people or that organizations and politicians are doing them favors. They do not believe in their power of agency. The partnership with SF allowed the *saladeros* to create a governance model, understand how to relate to other public and private stakeholders, and ensure their rights and interests. This is an important aspect of community partnerships, particularly with models such as this one. Because this approach intentionally engaged local residents, they created a new structure that became a civil society voice. It developed a new form of decision making beyond government that was more representative of the interests of the local population. This speaks to the importance of the nongovernmental sector and its potential to influence change, including revising various dimensions of local government. Both civil society and government substantially evolved as a result of this community partnership.

The thematic committees and governance model are still working in El Salado and the community continues to effectively advocate for other existing and new initiatives. For example, recently the sewage system was broken, and the community managed to contact the authorities to finance repairs. They know who to talk to and the procedures. Also, El Salado continues to work with partners in different projects. For instance, important restaurants and chefs like Crepes & Waffles and Harry Sasson continue to buy several products from El Salado. Creating state capacity allows communities to face crises like COVID-19. The experiences of El Salado demonstrate the potential of a community partnership to fundamentally transform democratic participation among residents and institutions as well as local governance in general.

The strategic design of this community partnership provides lessons that can be applied elsewhere. In partnership with IDB, SF designed and implemented similar methodologies for other areas in Colombia. However, in 2018 Semana, the media group who financed the salaries of the SF team, suffered an economic crisis. Due to this, SF stopped working on community-led initiatives.

## CHALLENGES AND LESSONS

This successful partnership did not advance and develop without challenges. People in El Salado were victims of the armed conflict in Colombia and of one of the most tragic massacres of the country. The collective trauma experienced by residents does not engender trust. In community partnerships, trust building is already time consuming. But in this instance, it was particularly difficult.

As noted, this partnership created a sense of agency among local residents. Culturally, this was a dramatic shift, as people were more accustomed to being beneficiaries of projects rather than active decision makers. This is a context in which government is expected to act, and the population seeks government's compliance. One of the most important challenges was to empower the community and individuals for them to feel entitled to act. Transforming the discourse from being victims forgotten by the state, to being citizens that are able to hold authorities accountable. It was also challenging to educate the community about navigating bureaucracy, in order to effectively communicate with the authorities and request what they needed.

This effort was covering new ground, as there were not many experiences of post-conflict and collective reparation in Colombia. This challenge was further magnified by the rural context. Social and economic inequality between urban and rural areas in Colombia is significant. El Salado is located in a poor rural area that was profoundly affected by the armed conflict. Connecting rural and urban stakeholders was challenging.

According to Claudia Garcia, the former director of SF, El Salado became a source of lessons to enterprises, governments, nongovernmental organizations, and other stakeholders interested in understanding the rural areas in Colombia and the challenges that they entail. El Salado allowed them to learn how to listen to communities, instead of planning their future from remote offices.[13] She suggested that communities must determine their own path, with the cooperation of other stakeholders in the public and private sectors. But we also must recognize the uniqueness of each community. No single model can be identically replicated in other areas affected by the conflict. Each reparation process is different and depends on the specific context of the community.

She also underscored that solutions should be created collectively without discharging full responsibility on the government. Repairing and rebuilding Colombia should be a collective effort involving schools, universities, enterprises, families, and citizens, among others.

Reparation and reconstruction entails coordination with multiple stakeholders. It is useless to build a public hospital if the state doesn't ensure that it has doctors. It is useless to create productive projects if there are no paved roads that allow the transportation of goods. Repairing communities is about creating circuits. In this sense, a community partnership can and should transcend narrow approaches to community and economic development that might address a single issue at a time, which is a more conventional approach by many nonprofits and foundations, including those in Colombia. With too heavy an emphasis on a specific issue, a project could fail to tackle the complex and intertwined dynamics of a community.

According to Garcia, repairing is not about executing projects. It is about enabling procedures. This involves change, commitment, empowerment, and cooperation. Reparation procedures shall aim to become autonomous and sustainable. This is an important point about the lasting potential of community partnerships. This is not only a matter of achieving a few quantifiable results in designated issues areas; community partnerships can alter methods of operating. This is to the benefit of the wide range of stakeholders in a given local ecosystem, because governments cannot do everything. Garcia thinks governments tend to have a more generic approach to projects. The timing, bureaucracy, and dynamics of government are sometimes not adaptable to communities. A coordinator like SF allowed local residents and other stakeholders to create sustainable and beneficial partnerships. This is another reason why the engagement of nonprofits and philanthropy in community partnerships is important. In El Salado, a space was created, beyond government, to enable creative solutions driven by civil society. This is a structure that did not exist before. It might not have existed at all without SF.

In Colombia and in communities having suffered from conflict, there is a lack of trust in the government and a feeling that governments owe people. They do not believe in their power of agency. Strengthening their leadership to interact with different stakeholders is a way to leverage the community's power of agency. Understanding how the government's agenda works, what documents and procedures should be developed, and how to ensure community rights is key.

It is important to build trust and create authentic relationships in community partnerships. The value of SF is that its team lived in El Salado, which allowed them to comprehensively understand the dynamics of the community, as well as their requests. Additionally, something special about having someone living in the community is that sometimes projects are suspended because of little details. Being able to identify the minor obstacles can ensure efficiency and effectiveness of the program. Keeping an eye on the little things is key. SF was able to do that.

Overall, SF's strategy in El Salado transcended the approach of most community partnerships, which tend to focus on collaboration across institutions. While this effort included numerous institutions, it also built in a more direct line of communication and connection with local residents. This was necessary given the context and crisis situation at hand. But it was integrated into the strategic approach, which was not only about rebuilding a devastated community, but transforming how the community functioned. This effort rearranged community-based agency, and ultimately created new accountability mechanisms between government and civil society.

## NOTES

1. www.ictj.org/sites/default/files/ICTJ-Colombia-Conflict-Facts-2009-English.pdf.
2. Centro de Memoria Histórica.
3. Centro de Memoria Histórica. La Masacre del Salado: Esta Guerra no era Nuestra.
4. https://colombiasupport.net/2011/06/montes-de-maria-power-land-and-violence/.
5. Centro Nacional de Memoria Histórica.
6. Semana Foundation is a nonprofit organization that works with the private sector, government, international cooperation agencies, and social organizations for social development projects.
7. Postales desde El Salado, la historia de un pueblo que reconstruyó a sí mismo.
8. Postales desde El Salado, la historia de un pueblo que reconstruyó a sí mismo.
9. Postales desde El Salado, la historia de un pueblo que reconstruyó a sí mismo.
10. M. Alejandra Cabal, interview, June 11, 2020.
11. Carulla Foundation is a nonprofit organization aimed at improving the coverage and quality of early childhood development services in Colombia.
12. Postales desde El Salado, la historia de un pueblo que reconstruyó a sí mismo.
13. Postales desde El Salado, la historia de un pueblo que reconstruyó a sí mismo, 13.

# 12. Malawi: Chipatala Cha Pa Foni

In Malawi 84% of the population lives in rural areas. Therefore, the nearest health-care center can often be hours away with an average consultation with a health-care consultant lasting just a couple of minutes. To resolve this huge issue of access to health care, international nongovernmental organizations (NGOs), local nonprofits, philanthropic foundations, a private telecom company, and local and national government agencies collaborated to develop Chipatala Cha Pa Foni (CCPF), which translates to "health center by phone." CCPF is a toll-free health and nutrition hotline which is in the process of transitioning from a localized, nonprofit-sponsored project to a national, government-led program. The development of CCPF represents a multistakeholder partnership which has undergone different stages of collaboration with some institutions purely engaged in the pilot period and others becoming more involved during the expansion of the program. The program was first piloted in the district of Balaka in 2011 with maternal, newborn, and child-care services, but then it was expanded nationwide to include all health topics.

The idea for CCPF was developed from a national campaign funded by the Bill and Melinda Gates Foundation soliciting strategies to address health challenges for improving maternal, newborn, and child health indicators, entitled "Share an idea, save a life." The concept originated by combining two winning submissions. In 2010, the initial concept derived from a software developer and district AIDS coordinator. It won a national campaign run by the Malawi Ministry of Health (MoH) and Concern Worldwide to identify challenges related to maternal care, child care, and malnutrition. Between 2011 and 2013, CCPF launched in Balaka district through VillageReach and Concern Worldwide. It expanded to two additional districts.

By 2016, the MoH officially endorsed CCPF. Telecom company Airtel declared a partnership with CCPF guaranteeing toll-free rates for Airtel users. CCPF ultimately expanded again to cover all general health topics and nutrition. Remote doctors were added for referrals. It also expanded to five more districts. The MoH signed a Memorandum of Understanding with Airtel to expand and manage CCPF at national scale by 2018. Major tech upgrades significantly expanded call center capacity. "CCPF for adolescents" launched, extending the platform to youth-friendly services and HIV prevention.

# THE PARTNERSHIP

CCPF was made possible through a strong partnership between fieldwork implementers, the MoH and the telecom industry that acted as active collaborators. In addition, several private organizations helped to fund the health initiatives implemented, each with a philanthropic role. Active collaborators in this effort include the following.

## VillageReach

VillageReach is a U.S.-based organization whose mission is to increase health-care access for underserved communities in low- and middle-income countries. It was created in 2001 and has 90 employees across all countries. It worked as the local nonprofit that nurtured the program from its pilot stages. It is the leading implementing partner in this initiative. As a nonprofit, its mission is to work with governments to solve health-care delivery challenges to low-resource communities. It specializes in filling the gaps of health systems that do not have the capacity to respond to demand in low-income countries playing a specific role in rural and remote communities. The mission is naturally aligned with the purpose of CCPF. Furthermore, VillageReach played a nonpartisan role as an honest broker between the government and private sector ensuring that all relevant stakeholders were on the same page in terms of CCPF's objectives. VillageReach could advocate for the initiative at the national and global levels. VillageReach's strong reputation in Malawi served as a "seal of approval" for Airtel when brokering the deal.

## Ministry of Health

As the original sponsor of the program, the MoH[1] provided overriding stewardship of the program's development. Struggling with the strain of health-care needs and issues of access, the MoH was focused on finding innovative solutions to these problems. Hotline workers were also trained in maternal, newborn, and child health using modules from the MoH's Health Surveillance Assistants curriculum. VillageReach recognized the importance of ministry-level buy-in and government champions for a successful scalability and sustainability strategy. MoH leadership gave the initiative legitimacy, and influenced other partners to become involved. Many countries prohibit over-the-phone diagnosis so this partnership provides a solid foundation for overcoming the legal and regulatory challenges a health hotline may face. Health outcomes were a priority government agenda. The MoH was well placed in its preparation to nationalize the program by setting the pace for scale and helping to identify internal and external stakeholders who could make the transition possible. Without internal advocates, scale-up would have been more challenging and time consuming. The MoH did not originally contribute direct funds to the project, but provided in-kind support such as hosting the hotline center at the Balaka District Hospital and providing staffing reinforcements.

**Balaka's District Health Management Team**

Balaka is a district in the southern region of Malawi. It has a population of over 310,000 and was the location in which the pilot program was first developed and so the local health-care team was essential in CCPF's development. It ensured optimum integration of CCPF into existing health services and generated local MoH leadership. It also allowed for a close relationship with local stakeholders which ensured that the project would remain community-oriented. The local health-care team was also crucial in terms of knowledge sharing and leveraging hospital resources. In terms of the former, nurses from district hospitals supervised hotline workers, staff brainstormed questions they thought a community member might ask when calling the hotline, and final content was reviewed by local women experienced in maternal and child health. They ensured that CCPF messages would adequately represent local traditions around pregnancy. In terms of the latter, space was provided for operating the hotline. This hospital-specific location enhanced the service's credibility as community members began to consider the hotline as an extension of the hospital.

**Concern Worldwide**

The original innovation of CCPF was funded by the Maternal, Newborn and Child Health (MNCH) initiative of Concern Worldwide,[2] a global humanitarian organization. This initiative was funded by the Gates Foundation (as part of a five year grant) in 2009 that aimed to develop creative solutions for improving the health and survival of mothers, babies, and children. Concern engaged with communities in the design process and worked with experts until a program was ready to be tried on a pilot basis. Concern contracted VillageReach to pilot the successful idea of CCPF. It analyzed data to determine the relative success of the program before selecting it for scale-up. After the pilot period of CCPF, Concern Worldwide Malawi incorporated the hotline into a broader project of strengthening health systems and overcoming barriers to access in the country. MNCH outcomes are a priority for the NGO and Concern was already working in focal districts. It went from implementing the program in one district to including nine more districts and, in addition to MNCH, the program added nutritional support, general health, and adolescent sexual reproductive health.

It promoted the service by leveraging volunteers to reach out to the community one person at a time, using radio ads and distributing posters and flyers.

**Baobab Health**

The nonprofit aims to lead the improvement of health through ICT in the developing world. It builds, deploys, and maintains innovative, robust, and sustainable health-care information systems in collaboration with government and health-care workers. It designed the touchscreen system used by CCPF workers that would work in the low-resource environment. Baobab provided the bulk of the technological support for the project and was involved in the transition to government and tech upgrades in 2018. CCPF paid Baobab for its services and this was an opportunity for Baobab to promote its own software and enhance its product.

**Airtel**

Airtel is one of two major telecommunications companies that operates in Malawi. It signed a Memorandum of Understanding with VillageReach and the MoH in 2015 which guaranteed that it would cover the cost of all incoming calls and promotional texts. As CCPF was developing and being piloted, Airtel was also building an mHealth program in Malawi called Dial-A-Doc. VillageReach and Airtel worked together to merge the two into a single service. Airtel's marketing strength has successfully promoted the service to people across Malawi. Without the Airtel partnership, the costs of nationalization might have prevented the government from taking full ownership. This was an opportunity to utilize Airtel's own platform for corporate social responsibility. Airtel benefited from the merger by leveraging VillageReach's expertise in program management and implementation as well as its health-care knowledge and content.

**United States Agency for International Development, Mobile Alliance for Maternal Action**

This is a public–private partnership for improving women's access to health care in the developing world through the use of mobile health technology launched in 2011 by the U.S. Agency for International Development. It was a key reference used by VillageReach when developing content for the CCPF tips and reminders service. It also helped create in-depth manuals and short, visual job aids for hotline workers to easily refer to during their calls.

## Community Organizations and Donors

Partnerships with local organizations working at the community level allow CCPF to address many of the barriers users face in accessing the service. Community actors promote the service and provide access to phones so users can call in. CCPF members also engage with health workers in rural health centers, building trust with health workers and patients. Donors have provided funding to expand the service in scope and scale, through content development, staff training, and infrastructure improvements, including moving the hotline call center from Balaka to a much larger and more technically advanced facility in Lilongwe (in 2018).

## Organized Network of Health Service Delivery for Everyone

This helped fund the national transition phase (salaries, costs for hotline including water, electricity, etc., and follow-up calls for referral tracking) and the relocation of the hotline and refurbishment of buildings. It also included technology upgrades, community mobilization in focal districts, and equipment in the new hotline building. It is a member of the Steering Committee.

## Innovations Work Group

VillageReach was awarded a grant to scale up the use of CCPF in Malawi by the United Nations Innovation Working Group's (IWG's) catalytic grant competition of maternal, newborn, and child mobile health, managed by Health Alliance. VillageReach was successful in the grant competition because it employed an effective delivery strategy for evidence-based maternal and child health intervention, combined with creative financing strategies to promote sustainability – elements that are critical for tools to contribute to Millennium Development Goals 4 and 5. Through IWG, VillageReach received specialized assistance from the World Health Organization's Department of Reproductive Health and Research to optimize the scale-up of CCPF while contributing to the mHealth evidence base and best practices on implementation and scale-up. These grants also provide the opportunity for collaborative learning among the grantees in their pursuit of health impact, financial sustainability, and scale. Through the grant, CCPF developed an expansion strategy which was to enter new districts by partnering with another nonprofit organization. The nonprofit helps to market the program and support program costs. For example, if 20% of the calls to the hotline came from a particular district, the nonprofit partner would help to pay for 20% of the costs of the program. Using the "district-by-district" strategy, CCPF expanded to 25% of districts in Malawi (United Nations Foundations, 2016).

**Vitol Foundation**

A funder since 2015, the Vitol Foundation has supported CCPF in scaling up the project to additional districts. It has also contributed funding for the program including technology and administrative costs to run the hotline.

**Seattle International Foundation**

This supported the expansion of health topics for the hotline as well as transition planning through the secondment of a technical assistant to the MoH.

**Viamo**

Viamo connects individuals and organizations using digital technology to make better decisions. In Malawi, in addition to the COVID-19 messages on the 3-2-1 service, it is also directing people to the CCPF call center if they need additional information. The call center is a partnership between the MOH, VillageReach, and Viamo.

**Johnson & Johnson**

The global health-care company donated funds to branding exercises. Through this service it was able to help ensure that the beneficiaries and stakeholders were able to collaborate on a set of brand principles. Partner brand visibility has proven to be important for multistakeholder initiatives. Johnson & Johnson also updated user guides and trained hotline workers to provide better customer service and improve the quality of advice. It has provided unrestricted funding for a number of key areas to support the scale-up and transition of the hotline to the MoH. It is involved in many areas of funding support, for example, the development of reference and professional training materials for the hotline, transition planning including support for the MoH's CCPF Steering Committee, the secondment of a technical adviser to the MoH to support transition planning, and branding. It supports areas that other donors were not funding which has been instrumental in terms of transition planning and scale-up.

**GSMA**

The industry organization represents the interests of mobile network operators worldwide. It was initially engaged through an advisory role (IWG) and then helped to broker the relationship with Airtel and provided funding for nutrition work. It provided credibility for the program within the mobile communications field.

## MECHANISMS FOR COLLABORATION

Several mechanisms were employed which guaranteed a successful collaboration. VillageReach deployed several focus groups to validate the messaging procedure to ensure the content was representative of the prominent health issues facing families in the rural Malawi context. Technical working groups were created as a way of developing relationships with the national level MoH. The Memorandum of Understanding defined the specific roles and responsibilities of each actor. Importantly, CCPF was always intended to become a government project and so the partnership strategy was successful due to the shared understanding of an ultimate goal. Contributions from strategic partners and individual donors support the infrastructure improvements and partnership development required for scaling. There was a steering committee led by the MoH, which Concern Worldwide attended.

## CHALLENGES FACED BY THE PARTNERSHIP

CCPF represents a complex partnership involving multiple partners with specific, mutually reinforcing roles. But among the various forms of collaboration from across the world integrated into the partnership, the idea is to reach an ultimate beneficiary population first in a single district in Malawi, and then in other communities. This is a community partnership intending to create a model for collaboration, coordination, and service delivery that can be implemented in other communities in the country with the support of the MoH.

Given the complexity of the arrangement, it is not surprising that various challenges surfaced. For example, as the project intends to connect to local communities to facilitate implementation, some relevant partners, such as traditional leaders and communal health workers, were not involved in actual implementation.

Growing a program of this sort is challenging in itself. Many additional consequences arise from growth. Airtel, in the face of increased call volume, was tasked with training additional staff. The MOH, in managing the hotline, required additional technical assistance for training to implement the program. This is a case in which local government is a central stakeholder. However, the level of government resources available must be taken into account. Initiatives such as CCPF are created in order to fill a void that cannot be served by government. Recognizing this reality, substantial ongoing resources are required to integrate new systems and services into local governments.

In a lower-income nation such as Malawi, the degree of existing infrastructure cannot be taken for granted either. CCPF depends on modern communication systems, such as mobile penetration, which is only 38% in Malawi. For fixed landlines, this figure is only 1.9%. Therefore, Airtel's role, which depends on mobile phones and landlines, requires the local growth of telecom in order to continue expanding the program at scale. Furthermore, in order to scale the program, CCPF needed to educate the public. Through the partnership with Airtel, CCPF created marketing and communication material, and it also advertised via SMS to Airtel subscribers, publicizing its services in new districts.

## IMPACT OF THE PROJECT

### 2018 Impact Evaluation

According to a 2018 Impact Evaluation,[3] compared to nonusers, the evaluation found that the CCPF users were more likely to:

- use antenatal care within the first trimester;
- use a bed net for children under five;
- have greater knowledge of the frequency for daily feedings of children under five;
- have received HIV testing in the last two years;
- have used a condom during their last sexual encounter, if unmarried;
- have used modern contraceptives in the past two years;
- have greater knowledge of post-exposure prophylaxis; and
- have greater knowledge of the importance of the six food groups.

Some indicators of impact in 2018 include:

- 92% of CCPF users had tested for HIV versus 82% of nonusers in the nine CCPF districts in the prior 24 months.
- 52% of unmarried CCPF users reported using a condom versus 29% of nonusers in the nine CCPF districts.
- 67% of CCPF users had used a (modern) contraceptive relative to 46% of nonusers in the nine CCPF districts.
- CCPF users were more informed than nonusers in the same communities (nine districts) about the existence of post-exposure prophylaxis drugs, a relatively new option for HIV prevention in Malawi.
- In terms of maternal health, 79% of CCPF users had planned pregnancy compared to 56% of nonusers.
- On child health 91% of all CCPF users' under-five children had slept under an insecticide-treated bed net to prevent malaria on the night preceding the

survey, compared to 88% of nonusers in their districts, and 77% of nonusers in four other districts.

- On nutrition 78% of CCPF users understood the importance of eating from all six food groups daily versus 54% of nonusers.

Clearly, this partnership can point to some specific indicators of success with an intended beneficiary population. It is a partnership that leveraged private philanthropy and partners across the public, private, and nonprofit sectors in order to develop a targeted approach to health service delivery in a developing African nation. All of these segments have played a crucial role in establishing and expanding a system with the intent to institutionalize a new approach into local government.

This type of community partnership raises questions about the availability of local assets. Whereas some urban areas in the U.S. might be able to build around anchor institutions, which are local assets in close proximity, in Malawi, we find a community partnership that relies on resources from a variety of sources locally. In this instance, global philanthropy has been playing an important and indispensable role. But philanthropy is ultimately catalytic as in many community partnerships in more developed contexts, such as the U.S., CCPF also builds on assets of hospitals. In particular, it extends beyond the physical site of a hospital, using telecommunications to reach a broader population, and leveraged a telecommunications company in order to expand capacity. CCPF also used expertise in public health to raise awareness. As is evident in the experiences of community partnership, if the intent is to reach underserved populations, important mechanisms must be instituted in order to build appropriate bridges between institutional partners and individuals or families. Community-based nonprofit organizations can play an important role in this regard. But in a context like Malawi, there is not a high degree of infrastructure among incorporated nonprofit organizations. These organizations might not truly represent civil society in the same way as traditional forms of community-based leadership. Community partnerships must remain continually cognizant of the unique dimensions of local contexts. This is especially true in a community partnership structured with numerous external stakeholders from many miles away.

## COVID-19 RESPONSE

VillageReach is advising the Malawi government on the best use of CCPF during the pandemic. Due to expected increased call volume, voice messages were implemented in the interactive voice response platform. This update, known as VillageReach and Focusing Philanthropy's COVID 411 campaign, builds on the existing infrastructure to provide timely and accurate health information during the COVID-19 crisis. Additionally, the health center by phone technology has been expanded to deliver remote, phone-based training to more than 100,000 health workers in Malawi and in other regions of focus.

As the CCPF hotline became overwhelmed, the government recruited and trained an additional 25 hotline workers to double capacity, as well as prepare for COVID-19 messaging in multiple languages.

VillageReach's COVID-19 response has been informed by the following principles:

1. Put government at the center. This can ensure that solutions reflect government priorities and support systems that are currently in place.
2. Build on what is known to work. VillageReach's response builds from its experience and existing solutions.
3. Collaborate and communicate. VillageReach aims to use these actions to inform communities about what it has to offer and how it can be supportive.
4. Respond to the present while designing for the future. Resilient, sustainable, and stronger systems should be created for current issues as well as post-pandemic functioning.

This is an example of how the infrastructure developed through a community partnership has been applied in a crisis. The capacity that was in place was not enough to handle the demand for calls, but the contours of the initiative were in place. This allowed them to expand on an existing framework. The COVID-19 response also illustrates how a community partnership catalyzed by philanthropy and built through cross-sector collaboration ultimately complemented, and extended, the impact of government.

## NOTES

1. Malawi's Ministry of Health aims to develop a sound delivery system capable of promoting health, preventing, reducing, and curing disease, protecting life, and fostering general well-being and increased productivity. Included among its objectives are expanding quality-of-health services for mothers and children under the age of five years.
2. Concern Worldwide is an organization that helps people living in extreme poverty achieve major improvements in their lives. To achieve this, they engage in long-term development work and respond to emergency situations.
3. Evaluation was funded by program donors; primarily Vitol Foundation and Johnson & Johnson.

# 13 England: young Black men's employment program in London – the Moving On Up initiative

In London in 2013, the employment rate for young Black men was just 56% compared to 81% for young white men. Even taking into account educational achievement, young Black men were far more likely to experience unemployment than their white counterparts. More than 83,000 young men in London are from Black and mixed Black ethnic groups. Trust for London (TfL),[1] having already worked with the Black Training and Enterprise Group (BTEG),[2] commissioned the nonprofit organization (or "charity") to conduct a feasibility study to determine specific barriers to employment for this population. According to the findings young Black men feel unsupported, and believe that racism and negative stereotyping are the main reasons for their high unemployment rate. A new community partnership developed, informed by the study and reality of these racial disparities.

## BACKGROUND ON THE PARTNERSHIP

The partnership between TfL and BTEG began in 2014, spurred by the airing of a BBC Panorama[3] television program focusing specifically on the disparity between young Black men and the rest of London's workforce in regard to employment rates. With the completion of the report, BTEG, in partnership with TfL and City Bridge Trust,[4] launched the first phase of the initiative entitled Moving On Up (MOU). This phase was focused primarily on skills training and employment support for participating young Black men and had six nonprofit providing partners. This phase lasted between 2015 and 2017. With its conclusion, the partners commissioned the Social Innovation Partnership[5] to conduct a report on the successes and challenges of the initiative. As a result of this report, MOU switched its focus to ensuring quality employment opportunities for participating young men. Quality employment is defined by paying the London Living Wage, providing professional development opportunities, and long-term advancement. Phase 2 (2018–present) involves multiple sites of collaboration including the Employers Champions groups which connect private-sector partners to the initiative, the Collective Impact Partnerships

(CIP) which sets up two local councils as the central source for service delivery to participants and fostering local partnerships, and work with the Greater London Authority[6] as part of its Workforce Integration Network.[7]

This partnership represents a break from traditional efforts by the "charity" sector to promote employment opportunities due to its specific focus on young Black men. While there have been a multitude of interventions with similar intentions, its focus has been on individual aspects of employability as opposed to an integrated, cohesive approach. Defying the conventional color-blind model, the partnership aimed to prove the importance of taking a demographic view to remedy inequalities in London's labor market. This effort is also another model of community partnership, which is highly focused on solving a particular problem with a single demographic group in the context of a very large city.

## STRATEGY

The initiative's original aim was to fund a cohort of organizations which would develop new ways of supporting young Black men into quality employment in a sustainable manner with the hope of influencing wider patterns in the labor market. In the first phase of the initiative, BTEG was the primary convener, with the financial support of TfL and City Bridge Trust, connecting participants with services and ensuring the feasibility of the projects through regular meetings of the London Advisory Group. Phase 2 of the initiative includes engaging with a wider array of sectors, involving a multitude of collaborative efforts with the aim of elevating the voices of all stakeholders and BTEG maintaining its position as the primary convener.

## MECHANISMS OF COLLABORATION

### Collective Impact Partnership

This model involves bringing together particular local stakeholders to agree and implement an action plan, and coordinating activities to improve employment outcomes for young Black men in two boroughs: Brent and Newham.[8] Both boroughs are places of high diversity and disadvantage, specifically around issues of low wage, and already engaged with connecting residents to local employers but not in an organized program. BTEG proposed unconstrained management funding to support an effort focusing specifically on employment opportunities to young Black men in the area. While the partnership has citywide intentions, it focused on two neighborhoods ("boroughs") in order to pursue demonstrable outcomes.

The partnership was formalized by monthly meetings, organized by the council, in which partners discuss progress, communication, and outreach. Three objectives guide the work of this partnership: improved employer engagement, improved outreach and engagement with young Black men, and increased opportunities for in-work progression for young Black men. Participants included funded delivery partners, BTEG, council services such as Job Brokers Services that can provide another perspective, Jobcentre Plus,[9] local universities, and employers. The composition of the partners highlights the complexity of a single issue of increasing employment outcomes for a particular demographic. The idea of changing employment outcomes for a historically underserved population requires the engagement of numerous institutions. Workforce development requires training as well as placement, but also a full understanding of and engagement with the population. These various levels require funding, particularly a long-term commitment.

The overall purpose of this partnership is to bring young Black men into quality employment. Therefore, participating stakeholders are invited to provide strategic input to achieve this goal. The expectation is that everyone in the borough can sit collectively, even if not directly funded by the project, and combine resources to initiate change collectively. This economy-of-scale model aims to test whether collaboration proves to be a better use of resources. CIPs have an evolving document called the Moving On Up Action Plan with input from all partners to ensure consensus. They embody the central role of relationship building in MOU's wider strategy.

**Employer Champions**

One lesson from the conclusion of Phase 1 was the need to properly engage with the private sector to ensure quality employment opportunities. The idea of the Employer Champions group was to target the industries that are most prominent in London and organize representatives in discussions around equitable hiring practices and employment conditions. Beginning with three industry groups (finance, construction, and technology) and ultimately merging into two (finance is now combined with construction) the Champions regularly meet to target issues and get feedback. The meetings' agenda is driven by the initiative director (BTEG). They are currently developing an employer toolkit informed by experience from interns, with the aim of improving messaging around these issues. The strategy of not merely providing employment opportunities but also engaging employers in long-term discussions around equitable practices serves to ensure the sustainability of the initiative's intentions.

## Ambassador Program

This was formed in 2020 as a way of involving young Black men in all aspects of the initiative. Nine ambassadors from across London were employed to provide input into the project and share their views on what key stakeholders could be doing to recruit, support, and progress people like them. Ambassadors work alongside Brent and Newham councils who are leading the CIPs. The ambassadors will provide insights and contribute to conversations about raising the profile of MOU in these boroughs and across London. They attend MOU Advisory Group meetings to shape the strategic direction of the initiative. Finally, they attend Employer Champions groups (tech and consulting/finance) to hear from employers. This is one model of how a community partnership can create direct pathways to engaging constituents beyond institutional collaborators.

## Influencing Policy

MOU is interested in expanding its initiative as something that can be embraced by local and national policymakers. During Phase 1, a London Advisory Group was established and received good engagement from the Department for Work and Pensions and the Greater London Authority, among others. Damian Hinds, minister of state for work and pensions, visited the MOU initiative in 2016, and there are ongoing conversations with the department about learning from MOU's targeted approach to supporting young Black men. Phase 2 involves extensive engagement with the Greater London Authority. As part of the "Strategy for Social Integration" the mayor launched the Workforce Integration Network to help improve pathways for under-represented groups in the workplace specifically focusing on young Black men (16–24 years old).

## THE PARTNERSHIP

### Main Collaborators

### Trust for London and City Bridge Trust
This provided £500,000 to six projects to support young Black men into employment. They spanned recruitment agency models, on-the-job experience, and group-based support to improve skills and build character. TfL originally commissioned the research that spurred the project between October 2013 and April 2014. In phase 2, TfL put an extra 2 million into the partnership. TfL also provides staff skills. Furthermore, the chair of the board has brought some of his employer connections and has been trying to find some employers to challenge their beliefs. This is an example of a philanthropic institution making

specific investments and remaining with the effort over a sustained period, and creatively identifying ways to engage employers.

### Black Training and Enterprise Group

This carried out research that informed the initiative's approach and convened initial stakeholders. Commissioned by TfL, research focused on why young Black men were faring less well in the labor market. This research helped to inform MOU's priorities. BTEG produced regular communications about MOU including press releases for the national, regional, and local media and briefing notes for interested groups. BTEG is the convening partner of the initiative and is the main conduit between the funders and the grantees. Given its historical focus on racial equity, it maintains considerable experience in reducing employment disparities. This experience ensures BTEG's success in coordinating the partners, performing project management with a racial equity lens, and holding partners accountable.

### Nonprofit Partners

Various nonprofit organizations handled different aspects of how to enhance job opportunities. Action West London,[10] as a recruitment agency, worked on a register for "job-ready" unemployed young Black men, helped improve their CVs and interview techniques, and advised during their search for and applying for jobs online. Step Ahead[11] used recruitment agency models, focusing directly on the skills required to successfully apply for jobs and brokering specific employment opportunities for young people. Elevation Networks[12] mixes group-based skills training with mentoring from employers. London Youth's Build-it Project[13] provides on-the-job work experience on a construction site, enabling young people to experience a work simulation (this was withdrawn from MOU earlier than planned because it was unable to scale up the Build-It project).

Beyond training and direct employment experience, nonprofits in the partnership also addressed other skills and competencies that are relevant in employment and careers. Making The Leap[14] provides group-based as well as one-to-one support focused on young people's skills, confidence, and outlook, focusing on emotional and social skills. Hackney CVS[15] (in partnership with SkyWay,[16] the Crib and Hackney Marsh Partnership) provides youth-led, community-based opportunities for young people to improve a range of skills and build character.

In the second phase of the partnership, which focused particularly on the boroughs of Newham and Brent, the funded partners had to compete for tender as groups moving Black and minority ethnic people into employment. In Newham, four partners joined together to compete: East London Business

Alliance,[17] A New Direction,[18] West Ham United Foundation,[19] and BAME 2020.[20] Overall, the partnership has been pursuing a comprehensive approach to enhancing employment opportunities for Black men and reducing disparities. It has been leveraging existing resources that were not coordinated around the particular common goal of greater employment for this particular population.

## IMPACTS

This initiative developed new ways of supporting young Black men into employment, by creating new pathways into employment and establishing strong links with employers and creating new opportunities. It led to a few successful employment outcomes for young Black men and had the potential to influence mainstream employment programs. According to an evaluation report on the effort, at least 271 (as many as 410) young Black men entered paid work following their participation in MOU. MOU had the biggest impact on participants' attitude, confidence, and understanding of work (Social Innovation Partnership, 2017). Through their assessments, MOU learned that participants most value that the staff cared and also appreciated when the projects were targeted and tailored to young Black men.

The report was also useful in directing the priorities of the second phase. Namely, the importance of engaging employers and engaging locally. The report states that "to meet an increased supply of high quality young Black male candidates, employers' demand must be increased too." This resulted in the formation of the Employer Champions groups. The report further recommends that "delivery could also benefit from more local engagement – maximizing enrolment into projects both by building networks among the local families and communities, and building relationships with Local Authorities," which explains the logic behind the CIPs.

But the depth of work required in order to meet the needs of a historically underserved community can never be underestimated. Funded projects, expected to engage with employers, struggled to dedicate the time needed to support the young Black men in as much depth as needed. TfL and City Bridge Trust are directly funding the CIPs over two years. In any jobs initiative, it is important to increase access to high-quality employment that can provide adequate compensation and benefits as well as career opportunities. This is the only way to truly transform deep and longstanding inequities. In some cases, the nature of employment secured by participants did not necessarily match applicants' qualifications.

MOU provides a compelling comprehensive model for connecting workforce development professionals, constituents (young Black men), various nonprofit organizations, philanthropic supporters, and employers. These are certainly relevant partners if the aim is to increase job opportunities for a particular demographic group. This strategic design contains some ideal elements in order to meet the partnership's goals, but actualizing the goal presents challenges. So many factors come into play in attempts to reduce racial disparities in employment because it is connected to numerous other concerns in education, housing, generational wealth, and other factors. The powerful impact of the COVID-19 pandemic on existing economic inequities only magnifies the challenge ahead. But this community partnership includes many of the elements that would be required to make a demonstrable impact on Black male employment. Future success will require a high level of commitment among partners, especially employers.

## NOTES

1. Trust for London is an independent charitable foundation that works to tackle poverty and inequality in London by funding charity groups, independent research, and providing expertise to policymakers and journalists. The trust from its endowed assets generates an income stream, which enables it to fund its work.
2. The Black Training and Enterprise Group is a national charity that started in 1996 and delivers programs for young Black, Asian, and minority ethnic (BAME) people. The organization conducts action research, operating as a learning partner for funders and providing a voice to government for BAME organizations. It is a networking organization supporting over 1,200 voluntary groups and community businesses in England.
3. BBC Panorama is an investigative documentary series from the United Kingdom.
4. City Bridge Trust is the funding arm of Bridge House Estates. It was established to make use of funds surplus to bridge requirements and provides grants totaling around £25 million per year towards charitable activity. It works to reduce inequality and grow stronger, more resilient, and thriving communities for a London that serves everyone.
5. The Social Innovation Partnership is an advisory social business to central and local governments, leading foundations and charities and private-sector organizations. Through a citizen-centered design approach they drive cross-sector engagement to deliver transformational change and enable clients to secure economic and social value.
6. The Greater London Authority is a top-tier administrative body responsible for the strategic administration of Greater London.
7. The Workforce Integration Network of the Greater London Authority is the mayor's initiative to improve pathways for under-represented groups in the workplace. The program supports young Black men aged 16 to 24 years into living wage employment in London.
8. There are five types of local authority in England: county councils, district councils, unitary authorities, metropolitan districts, and London boroughs. In this case, Brent and Newham are both London boroughs that work as unitary authorities. However, the Greater London Authority provides London-wide government and shares responsibility for certain services.

9. Jobcentre Plus is a government-funded employment agency overseen by the Department of Work and Pensions. Its purpose is to help people find work through services such as job-hunting programs and external job vacancies, while it also provides financial support to eligible job hunters.

10. Action West London is a London charity, a limited company that has worked with private-sector agencies across west London to secure education, training, and employment for unemployed young people and adults since 1998.

11. Step Ahead is a London-based recruiting company and training agency.

12. Elevation Networks was a youth employment charity that developed the leadership potential in talented young people aged 11–25, focusing on groups that were traditionally under-represented. The organization partnered with employers to create diverse career opportunities, but no longer exists as of May 2020.

13. London Youth is a charity that works to improve the lives of young people in London.

14. Making The Leap is funded to deliver Moving On Up to young Black men across London. The Moving On Up project is a social mobility charity, funded by Trust for London and City Bridge Trust to help young Black men into employment.

15. Hackney CVS is a local organization that supports the engagement of community groups, charities, and voluntary organizations with residents of Hackney. It acts as a bridge between the public sector and local community groups.

16. SkyWay works with some of the most vulnerable young people offering practical and emotional support through a wide range of activities and programs in youth clubs, local sports centers, parks, housing estates, and on the streets.

17. The East London Business Alliance builds the connection between businesses and local communities, bringing the time, skills, and resources of the private sector to help build the capacity of local organizations, support young people in education, and place people into employment in London.

18. A New direction is a London-based nonprofit, generating opportunities for children and young people to unlock their creativity.

19. West Ham United Foundation is an independent charity that works with community outreach organizations providing inclusive, life-changing opportunities for residents in east London and Essex.

20. BAME 2020 is an organization that aims for 20% of all marketing and communications professionals to come from a Black, Asian, minority ethnic background.

# 14  India: Parivartan – health in Bihar

Bihar, one of India's most densely populated states, with a population close to 100 million, is one of the poorest states in the country with high rates of maternal and newborn mortality and low literacy rates. Ninety percent of residents live in rural areas leading to acute challenges surrounding health-care access, including maternal health. Bihar has the highest fertility rate in India with an unmet need for contraception at 38%. Accounting for 8% of India's population and 10% of its annual births, Bihar contributes to 12% of maternal deaths, 12% of neonatal deaths, 13% of non-fully immunized children, and 15% of underweight children (Rangarajan et al., 2011).

## BACKGROUND ON THE PARTNERSHIP

The connection between poverty and poor maternal health led to a 2010 partnership between the government of Bihar and the Gates Foundation to accelerate improvements in a range of priority health outcomes. The Gates Foundation had set a focus on improving the lives of India's poor and marginalized, helping the country to get the best results possible from its investments. Since the government of Bihar prioritized health care for mothers and children, and the Gates Foundation was already working in Bihar, the partnership was created. The aim was to reduce maternal, newborn, and child mortality; malnutrition; fertility; and morbidity from infectious diseases by developing and implementing innovative and integrated health solutions that involve both the public and private sectors. The Ananya Initiative, with a grant worth $100 million, would fund a range of complementary pilot projects from 2010 to 2015 in eight select districts with the aim of improving health services and shaping health demands in Bihar. This program was in itself a multisector project. Within the broader effort, there is much to be learned from a single pilot project, *Parivartan*, the Bihar Community Mobilization Project.

Parivartan is a grant project as part of Ananya which focuses primarily on fostering community mobilization and social accountability. It aims to provide a platform of empowerment for women in the pilot districts to catalyze support networks, and enable behavioral shifts to reach health and sustainable health outcomes. Such platforms are developed in the form of a community self-help group consisting of around 12 to 15 women. At the grassroots level, these groups are managed by village volunteers known as *Sahelis* who play a critical role as conduits of information for the target women. Selected for their leadership and communication skills, Sahelis are trained on key maternal and child health and sanitation issues. For example, they established a nurse-mentoring program that has doubled the number of nurses who wash their hands and wear gloves before and during procedures.[1] This reliance on Sahelis is a form of how a community partnership can develop pathways to enhance reach at the grassroots level.

## STRATEGY

According to the Gates Foundation, the intent of this initiative is to bring about innovative solutions to improving the quality and coverage of key services. For example, helping frontline workers with healthy practices like breastfeeding, the Foundation developed teaching aids based on digital technology.

The goal of Parivartan is to promote healthy behaviors among participating women regarding maternal, newborn and child health (MNCH) and to improve their access to health-care services by facilitating linkages with frontline health workers, strengthening accountability. Parivartan represents one of eight community partnerships that are leveraged by substantial philanthropic resources from an external foundation. It incorporates strategies to connect a health-care infrastructure to populations that are disconnected from resources and education that can improve their health and well-being. But getting this information to the villages requires direct engagement and collaboration with volunteers in those areas.

## NONGOVERNMENTAL/NONPROFIT ORGANIZATIONS IN THE PARTNERSHIP

The Bill and Melinda Gates Foundation provides the bulk of the funds in this initiative and thus plays a primary role from a philanthropic perspective. Acknowledging the limited role it can play in an ecosystem dominated by the state and national government, the Gates Foundation focuses primarily on providing strategic support to partners, either through seed funding, working on research and development, or bringing partners from different sectors together.

As an international nonprofit, Project Concern International's (PCI) mission is to empower people to enhance health outcomes. In 2013, PCI developed Women Empowered, a global initiative designed to promote the social and economic advancement of women. PCI is unique in its integration of social development activities into its core objectives and has successfully developed a system to foster self-help groups through this initiative. As a result, PCI was chosen as the lead partner in the Parivartan initiative and was responsible for the overall program implementation having received $15 million from the Gates Foundation to help improve sanitation and MNCH in Bihar. PCI leads community-based action which is being implemented by eight local nongovernmental organizations (Nida, Vikas, etc.) and conducts district-wide interventions to foster and strengthen community groups. PCI also helped develop training modules used by Sahelis as part of the Parivartan compendium. Additionally, in collaboration with Google, PCI built a mapping system to show the location of villages served by the Parivartan project with corresponding project data to enhance the efficiency of the initiative.

PATH is a global nonprofit working to accelerate health equity by serving as the technical advisory partner in the Parivartan project. PATH helped develop the training modules as part of the Parivartan compendium and worked through self-help groups to provide women with health tips on pregnancy, childbirth, family planning, etc. PATH was uniquely positioned to use data from the program to inform the government's plan to increase the scale of the initiative and create 1 million self-help groups in the state. It conducted surveys of 3,800 group members, sifted data, and broke it down geographically to find increases in key health educators. PATH also conceptualized the village entry and group formation process in consultation with the consortium partners, creating a training framework on this process.

The Foundation for Research in Health Systems (FRHS), also a nonprofit organization, is committed to a research and evidence-based approach to improving public health services in India. It works to strengthen existing health systems through evaluating ongoing programs and identifying gaps in existing policies. In the Parivartan project, FRHS guided the community-based action stream on proven models and interventions so that stakeholders could achieve a sustained impact across Bihar.

## GOVERNMENTAL ORGANIZATIONS IN THE PARTNERSHIP

The government of Bihar has been prioritizing health care for mothers and children for over a decade. As the third biggest state, Bihar's public health system consists of hundreds of thousands of workers from doctors to frontline workers. The government plays a key role in scaling up successful pilot initiatives to go beyond original target districts. But efforts to improve the health situation in Bihar are hampered by health system weaknesses, including gaps in infrastructure and demands for appropriate reproductive and MNCH services.

The Bihar Rural Livelihoods Promotion Society (Jeevika) is a program of the government of Bihar for poverty alleviation. The core strategy is to build vibrant community institutions of women that could be self-managed with member saving, internal loans, and economic activities, commonly known as self-help groups. Jeevika signed a Memorandum of Cooperation with Parivartan, which indicated that Parivartan would help Jeevika advance a health, water, and sanitation agenda with these community institutions and Parivartan community groups would transition to become incorporated into the Jeevika framework. Parivartan trained Jeevika's Sahelis while Jeevika supported the training of Parivartan's block and community coordinators. PCI furthered this partnership in providing technical assistance to build institutional capacity with the aim of developing a scalable Jeevika model that would promote MNCH practices.

## THE UNIQUE VALUE OF NONGOVERNMENTAL/ NONPROFIT ORGANIZATIONS IN THE PARTNERSHIP

Each partner fulfilled a specific purpose to ensure the sustainability and development of the initiative. The Gates Foundation's substantial resources and broad international and intersectoral reach facilitated the dual function of a funder and convener, providing significant seed money as well as bringing partners together. Indeed, the Gates Foundation is an outlier in philanthropy, as the wealthiest of all philanthropic institutions, but their experience in Parivartan speaks to some of the unique ways in which foundations can contribute to community partnerships. Certainly, financing is very important; and Gates has much to give. However, the convening power is particularly valuable with respect to partnerships. Community partnerships are strategically designed to solve problems in particular localities and/or regions. But bringing the right partners to the table in order to collaborate can be challenging and labor-intensive. It can also be quite time consuming, as potential partners must learn to identify common interests and work together. They must also transcend their own institutional interests and priorities. The engagement of a foundation such as Gates can accelerate the complex process of convening partners. If the Gates Foundation makes a request, especially among nonprofit organizations, people respond.

PCI is unique in its integration of social development activities into its core objectives and has successfully developed a system of self-help groups through this initiative. PCI, as the lead partner, plays the role of a hub through which other partners connect. This is a crucial role in all community partnerships, because ultimately, a partnership becomes an entity in itself. An institution must, in effect, embody the partnership. PATH was uniquely positioned to support the technical aspects of this initiative, developing resources that ranged from training modules to providing a scale-up plan for the government. PATH, in many ways, acts as an expert partner, bringing technical knowledge and expertise. FRHS provides ongoing evaluation of programs and policies, strengthening health systems by identifying gaps. Indeed, the need to assess progress and ensure that the initiative is continually learning and improving is another significant role.

## IMPACT

Jeevika signed a Memorandum of Cooperation with Parivartan which mandated that Parivartan would help Jeevika advance a health, water, and sanitation agenda with these community institutions and Parivartan community groups would transition to become incorporated into the Jeevika framework. Parivartan trained Jeevika's Sahelis while Jeevika supported the training of Parivartan's block and community coordinators. PCI furthered this partnership in providing technical assistance to build an institutional capacity with the aim of developing a scalable Jeevika model that would promote MNCH practices. Up to 2013, Parivartan had reached out to 280,000 women of reproductive age, through 18,000 community groups, in approximately 2,250 villages. The groups are supported by 2,600 Sahelis.

It is important to note that Parivartan's success is contingent on collaboration with other initiatives as part of the Ananya program. One such initiative was implemented by BBC Media Action, which focuses on shaping demands and practices, using communication in nontraditional ways that combine mass media, mobile phones, community mobilization, and interpersonal communication to extend health information and advice to rural populations. CARE[2] has worked to strengthen facilities by increasing availability, quality, and coverage of key family health interventions. Care, BBC Media Action, and PCI work together closely, leveraging each other's support.

As in rural Africa, the local ecosystem in rural India contains fewer resources than would be found in an urban context. Therefore, the ecosystem that is leveraged in order to solve a local problem is essentially national and global. An effort such as Parivartan, focused on a few rural villages in India, is drawing upon the Gates Foundation and other nonlocal partners along with government to influence health outcomes among women in the villages. This form of community partnership makes a resource leap. It stretches beyond the locality to draw in resources from elsewhere. These partners from elsewhere may or may not have a vested interest in the particular locality. However, a mission-driven organization might. This is another reason why the involvement of philanthropy and nongovernmental organizations is so important in the process of collaboration to solve problems in localities. The nonprofit organizations involved in Parivartan along with the Gates Foundation are pursuing their missions through their involvement in this initiative. This is a more reliable arrangement, in most cases, than a partnership focused primarily on the resources of private corporations.

In community partnerships, it is important to strike the right balance between purpose and interest. Stakeholders in partnerships need incentives to remain involved, especially over lengthy periods. They must continually justify their participation. Therefore, the nature of the central interests of stakeholders is an important factor to consider. Nonprofit organizations and philanthropic institutions can be connected to community partnerships through mission alignment. Community partnerships to improve public health, such as Parivartan, can bring together a collection of organizations with an existing interest in public health. This can certainly be the case in public–private partnerships as well, as participating corporations could be gathered based on either an interest in the geographical location and its population or an interest in health. A pharmaceutical company, for example, could be an active partnership in solving health problems. But in the nonprofit sector and in philanthropy, potential partners could include various organizations with a primary interest, embedded in the mission, in population health.

## NOTES

1. Gates Foundation.
2. CARE India is a not-for-profit organization that has worked in India for 70 years, focusing on the empowerment of women and girls.

# 15. Australia: Metropolitan partnerships – Victoria

With more than 5.3 million inhabitants, Victoria is the second most populous state in Australia. For the Victorian government, public participation plays a central role in government decision making and developing effective strategies, programs, and projects. According to the Victorian Auditor Generals Office,[1] public participation is embedded or supported in key pieces of Victorian legislation because it makes good sense and is consistent with a system where governments spend public funds to benefit the community.

The Victorian government wants to better understand and respond to the needs of Melbourne's communities. Over the next 30 years, Melbourne is projected to become Australia's largest city, nearly doubling its population. One important challenge amidst this rapid growth will be to ensure that the suburbs are equipped for the future.

The Metropolitan Partnerships are advisory groups established by the Victorian government in 2017. This approach is a coordinated way for metropolitan communities to advise government on local issues and opportunities in their region. These partnerships provide a pathway for local communities to engage directly with state and local governments, and to provide input to the Victorian government regarding priorities for jobs, services, and infrastructure across the region. Becoming a member of the Metropolitan Partnerships presents a new opportunity to collaborate with the community and government and positively shape the outcomes of a representative region. These partnerships, bringing together all levels of government, community, and business, are designed to make Victorian suburbs healthier, more resilient, and thriving places to live and work.

This approach relies less on specific nonprofit organizations in order to directly engage civil society. This is more of a direct linkage between government and particular local populations. In order to enable focused approaches in subsets of a large, populous region, the model is established in various localities in the broader geographical area. This ultimately creates a series of community partnerships that are applying a similar framework. They have in common a structured line of communication with the Victorian government.

# STRATEGY

Six Metropolitan Partnerships are active across Melbourne: Inner Metro, Inner Southeast, Western, Northern, Eastern, and Southern. Each partnership comprises eight community and business representatives, the chief executive officer of each local government in that region, and a deputy secretary from the Victorian state government.

Community and business members were recruited to the Metropolitan Partnerships through a public expression of interest process. Potential candidates submitted applications, and shortlisted applicants were interviewed. Forty-eight successful candidates were chosen, including the chairs and deputy chairs, from over 170 applications. This is an open model, which does not predetermine representatives from the community at large. Interested parties can apply. This is an intriguing approach, relying on self-selection to a degree in order to identify participants.

The Metropolitan Partnership model follows four phases. The partnerships facilitate annual planning and community engagement activities each year, and submit formal advice to the government through the minister for suburban development. Phase 1 of the partnership model involves meetings and engagement. Throughout the year, the partnerships work with their communities to identify opportunities for driving improved social, economic, and environmental outcomes. They coordinate with regional stakeholders, government departments and agencies, and regional leadership groups, and engage directly with communities. Phase 2 includes annual community engagement. Every year, the partnerships engage with the community to explore, test, and refine priorities for their respective regions. This provides the partnership with annual advice for the government. In Phase 3, the partnerships submit their annual advice to government on regional outcomes and priority initiatives for the coming year. Phase 4 involves the government's coordinated response. The minister for suburban development works with portfolio ministers to respond to the partnerships' advice. Responses can occur through existing programs and services, supporting further investigation of issues using Metropolitan Partnerships Development Funds, and new initiatives funded as part of the annual state budget process.

One of the six examples of this model is the Eastern Metropolitan Partnership, which includes the local government areas of the Yarra Ranges Council, Maningham City Council, Maroondah City Council, City of Knox, City of Whitehorse, and City of Monash. The partnership members include up to nine community and business representatives, the chief executive officers of each local council in the region, and a senior executive representing the Victorian government. The partnership's 2018 activities included contributing to the metropolitan-wide Youth Forum to bring youth voices from the east to the table, and hosting an annual assembly to bring together 68 community members, councilors, mayors, and government ministers.

The partnership also conducted a business forum attended by 30 employers in transport, social housing, environment, business, community health, youth, and sport sectors. This forum developed the following priorities for business: improved transport connections, as well as improvements to the road and freight network to support the regional economy; support for young people with better skills and training to ensure they are better prepared for joining the regional workforce; and affordable housing and improved public transport services to assist with workforce retention. The partnership's inclusion of direct engagement with employers alongside coordination with interested individual participants from local communities demonstrates a dynamic strategic design. The partnership model serves as an ongoing feedback loop, bringing local insights into the Victorian government from various sources. As this is a governmental partnership, it also represents a compelling approach to participatory democracy.

The partnership's 2018 priorities focused on improving management of the region's growth and on addressing critical regional issues. From the annual assembly, the following top three priorities were chosen: environmental sustainability; affordable and social housing; and social inclusion. Students and young people who attended the Youth Forum chose the following priorities: education – including life skills in the school curriculum and connecting schools with higher education environment sustainability – protection and education, and the promotion of renewable energy; mental health – improving services and increasing awareness in schools and the broader community; and public safety – improving security, especially for women, in areas such as transport hubs.

The partnership's advice to the government focused on five aspects:

1.  *Regional connectivity*: the partnership's desired outcome is for improved transport connections to make it easier to get around the region and improved access to the region's natural assets. Based on community input on this topic, the partnership's proposal to the government included a suggestion for investment in an integrated network of active transport infrastructure which is well connected to public transport. The government has responded by committing to provide better walking and cycling infrastructure and by including investment provisions in the Victorian budget 2019–2020 towards new parkland areas that include new walking and bike trails across Melbourne.

2.  *Integrated health and social services*: the partnership's desired outcome is for the region's most vulnerable people to have local access to the full

range of health and social services that they need. Community input led the partnership to propose an innovative health and social service delivery model pilot, which would prepare for the development of a trial in the outer eastern region. With the Department of Health and Human Services, the partnership has engaged Easter Health to deliver the project using $85,000 in seed funding from the Metropolitan Partnerships Development Fund.

3.  *Social inclusion*: the partnership's desired outcome is for all people in the region, regardless of age, gender, cultural background, or physical ability, to feel a sense of connectedness and have opportunities to participate in community life. Community input led the partnership to propose gender equality and unconscious bias in a training module trial at a selection of sporting clubs across the Eastern region. The government has responded by implementing a range of initiatives that support gender equity in sport, including the Manningham Inclusive Clubs program, among others.

4.  *Affordable social housing*: the partnership's desired outcome is for all people in the region to have a safe and affordable place to live. They proposed new social housing developments to deliver a minimum of 11,420 social housing dwellings to the Eastern region by 2036, including 910 dwellings for people with disabilities. One government response was that the Victorian budget 2019–2020 allocated $209 million to deliver 1,000 new public housing dwellings across Victoria, including in the city of Stonnington.

5.  *Jobs for youth*: the partnership's desired outcome is for an improvement in the transition from secondary school to meaningful training or employment for young people in the region. The partnership proposed research to better understand the overlap, duplication, and gaps in direct employment and training services offered in the region. The Department of Education and Training is collaborating with the partnership and the Outer Eastern Local Learning and Employment Network to deliver a Metropolitan Partnerships Development Fund project that develops an evidence base to quantify such overlap, duplication, and gaps.

## A CONTINUOUS ADVISORY MECHANISM

The partnerships transcend singular moments to solicit community feedback. The initiatives are institutionalized. Each year, the partnerships identify priorities for their region. They bring people from the community, industry, and government together at an annual assembly, to harness the feedback and ideas from local communities. The partnerships had an inaugural annual assembly in 2017 through which community members could take part in person or by joining the conversation at Engage Victoria. Engage Victoria is the Victorian government's online consultation platform provided by the state of Victoria through the Department of the Premier and Cabinet and supported by Harvest Digital Planning. The partnerships also work with regional and local groups, networks, and organizations to progress and develop local responses to issues. Clearly, the use of digital platforms provides additional communication streams between the government and local populations.

These priorities are presented to the Victorian government through the minister for suburban development. This independent advice informs key decision-making processes and enables government to be more responsive to community needs and better target its investment. The Metropolitan Partnerships are also now establishing five-year plans for each of the suburbs. Long-range planning adds another dimension to the partnership model.

## COVID-19 REALITIES AND BEYOND

The COVID-19 pandemic has highlighted the value of coordination and collaboration across sectors in localities. Many of the community partnerships featured herein were leveraged in order to help their communities navigate the great challenges presented by the pandemic. In 2020, the Metropolitan Partnerships worked on "living locally." This aim highlighted understanding the impacts of COVID-19 and future opportunities for recovery at the local level, as the pandemic has caused persons to experience their neighborhoods and communities in new and different ways. The Victorian government collected survey information to explore current impacts, support for communities, and recovery in the future. The information will help local planning for the future, particularly to address the economic and social impacts of COVID-19.

In this instance, the Metropolitan Partnerships model was a useful tool to inform government planning based on community experiences. Overall, the Victorian government has developed an instructive framework for ongoing participatory governance. The Metropolitan Partnerships' design does not rely on private philanthropy, distinguishing this approach from other community partnerships featured herein. The other partnerships in this book are filling voids unfilled by government. But, similar to the other featured community partnerships, Metropolitan Partnerships transcend sectors and involve civil society in local governance. Nonprofit organizations represent a third sector, beyond government or the private sector, to serve as a voice of civil society. The Victorian government is engaging civil society through interested individual partnerships. It is also engaging the private sector, but through organized businesses.

Overall, community partnerships beyond the U.S. are typically not operating in contexts with robust nongovernmental sectors. Their structures and approaches vary significantly. In lower-income countries, community partnerships might require outside resources (philanthropy from afar, for example) in order to function. But all of these partnerships leverage assets within a local ecosystem of organizational and human resources. Community partnerships are contextual. They are reflections of their surroundings. In some cases, they emerge due to limited government capacities. In other cases, they are actually led and created by government. Whereas community partnerships without some alignment with local government are plentiful in the U.S., it is much more difficult to find such models beyond the U.S.

One feature that stands out among international community partnerships is the range of creative approaches to reaching grassroots groups in civil society. These partnerships are intentionally seeking to connect broadly, in some instances, to the most vulnerable community residents. In some instances, they created liaisons to these communities; in others, they constructed direct lines of collaboration and communication. These partnerships are less institutional, as broader populations in civil society might more likely engage beyond incorporated organizations. Perhaps with the presence of established nonprofit organizations representing particular communities, these lines of communication and collaboration might be less direct to local populations.

What is clear across the U.S. and other parts of the world is that community partnerships are important mechanisms to solve problems in localities. They may take different forms, but they emerge from the realization that certain parties should collaborate in order to improve their localities. Philanthropy and nonprofit organizations have played a vital role in facilitating the emergence of these formations. This is not always the case, but any party can identify the need for and potential of community partnerships. Strategically, community partnerships have become pathways to local solutions.

## NOTES

1. The Victorian Auditor Generals Office plays a key role in promoting confidence in the public sector and created a "Public participation in government decision-making" guideline for Victorian government agencies.

# PART IV

# Lessons and the future

# 16.  Introduction to Part IV

Community partnerships are distinct from traditional conceptions of public/private partnerships. Community partnerships are uniquely contextual. They are comprised of various institutions emerging from a locality's particular ecosystem of organizations across sectors. Community partnerships tend to include some variation of types of nongovernmental organization.

A partnership between a government agency and a large corporation tends to have some focused utility, often through a transactional arrangement. For example, the U.S. government partners with SpaceX to launch rockets. The U.S. government benefits from SpaceX's expertise, helping to continue advancing space exploration. SpaceX receives funding from the U.S. government, and gains an opportunity to use its spacecraft for broader purposes that receive substantial exposure.

Mutual benefit is also fundamental to community partnerships. But community partnerships are focused on strengthening localities. They are driven by social purposes in order to reduce inequality, improve health, enhance a local economy, or some other end that impacts the quality of life in a geographic area. Furthermore, community partnerships are not restricted to any particular sector. The idea of public/private partnerships (at least in a literal sense) overlooks the nonprofit/nongovernmental sector. Nonprofit organizations are fundamental to community partnerships.

These various characteristics are reflected in the community partnerships featured in this book. They are collaborative initiatives designed to solve local problems. They both fill voids that government may not be able to handle as well as creatively innovate well beyond government's expectations. These community partnerships represent new forms of governance that harness resources and expertise that are dispersed across an array of local organizations in different fields of work. Therefore, organizations participating in community partnerships are reflective of their surroundings.

The composition of these collaborative efforts includes enduring local organizations – anchor institutions. These anchor institutions, because of their longevity in their localities, maintain an ongoing vested interest in the future of their communities. The partnerships come together out of some common interest in improving their localities partly due to the interdependence of a range of organizations in a given area's institutional ecosystem.

Community partnerships take on lives of their own. They are challenging to maintain over time, because they are tasked with galvanizing and sustaining interest and engagement across numerous different priorities. While organizations share an interest in the future of their communities, they each have specific priorities. The community partnerships in this book, given these complex dynamics, face a number of challenges. But these partnerships continue to proliferate in various communities, because they are ultimately necessary.

It is important to note that these partnerships are facilitated by democratic contexts. They are based on a certain degree of civic engagement and a sense of civic responsibility among institutions. In societies that do not promote these values, it is more difficult for these efforts to thrive. A democratic society will promote the presence of a robust nongovernmental sector, which represents civil society.

The U.S. context has been conducive to community partnerships partly because of the nonprofit/nongovernmental sector, which happens to rely on philanthropy for its survival, but also its independence from government. Cross-sector community partnerships are becoming increasingly common in the U.S. This book includes examples of community partnerships beyond the U.S. as well in order to illustrate how these collaborative formations can develop in other contexts.

This book featured a highly varied array of community partnerships. The manifestations of these efforts are reflections on their national and local contexts. But there are common themes regarding partnerships' effectiveness and shortcomings. Overall, they are strategic almost by design. They are created in order to bring about complex solutions, and are faced with multiple options regarding their composition, goals, and tactics.

# 17.  Successes and challenges

## REMAINING MISSION-DRIVEN

Considering how these partnerships achieve success, effective community partnerships are mission-driven. With a sense of a defined mission, community partnerships have clear goals and a mutual set of beliefs among partners. This enables smoother working processes with less incidence of conflicting priorities. Indeed, conflicting priorities are always present, but successful partnerships leverage a clear mission in order to transcend competing interests. Effective partnerships not only convene institutions around mutual interests, they design their work in service of partners' commonalities.

Successful mission-driven partnerships also emphasize:

- Inclusive, holistic, diverse, equitable development strategies.
  - They link economic inclusion to capital and/or broader community development initiatives; fostering entrepreneurial opportunities and promoting access to capital and markets for underserved populations.
- Civic engagement: fostering community mobilization, social accountability, and leadership.
  - They create public spaces for community members to learn about, respond to, and inform key issues of concern. This includes creating leadership opportunities for stakeholders in the community. Overall, these partnerships incorporate grassroots-level engagement into their work.
- A diverse blend of partners in their composition.
  - This allows different levels/sectors of societal groups to be reached. The greater the number of types of partners included, the more a partnership can represent its local ecosystem. Partnerships must be able to harness the unique experiences of institutions across sectors. Engaging local governments can be particularly important in order to influence lasting impact in areas such as local economic development.
- Targeting particular structural and contextual barriers.
  - These could include improving the quality and coverage of health services or improving access to health-care services by facilitating linkages with frontline health workers. For example, these partnerships

target racial disparities in economic well-being and wealth inequalities – areas of historical inequity that have created persistent challenges in their communities. Income disparity by gender or historical disinvestment in communities of color (or other historically disenfranchised groups depending on the context) are fundamental examples of obstacles to progress in localities and regions.

- Accountability between institutions, partners, communities, and other stakeholders.
  - Mission-driven community partnerships are committed to the goals they have established. They seek to measure impact, and demonstrate the value of their collective pursuits. They reflect on their efforts and discuss their limitations.
- A shared understanding of the ultimate goal of their work.
  - The pathway to success for community partnerships is seldom linear. Partnerships must be able to adapt and make mid-course corrections toward an ultimate goal or set of goals. By keeping ultimate goals in mind, partnerships are able to remain true to their mission even while assessing and altering tactics if necessary. The COVID-19 pandemic is a clear example of a contextual factor that forces new thinking and approaches to achieve goals.

Beyond the significance of mission-driven approaches in community partnerships, success is demonstrated in other ways as well, including the following.

## Integrating Community-Driven Development Initiatives/Local Engagement

To varying degrees, these partnerships place communities at the forefront of decision making, goal setting, and benefits. Whatever the particular structure, the nature of their work aims to benefit communities directly. This is part of the unique value of community partnerships, which are based on the idea that pressing social and economic challenges are experienced at the community level. In order to adequately impact these challenges, community partnerships must leverage resources across a variety of different types of institutions and build clear bridges to the neighborhoods in communities that are in the most need.

As many of the featured partnerships are based on the participation of institutional stakeholders, it is important to consider the degree to which these formations actually engage grassroots constituents. The U.S.-based partnerships highlighted herein are generally more institutionally based than those in other countries. These U.S. initiatives are based in urban areas, and founded on the idea of leveraging the resources of significant local employers – anchor institutions – and other organizations that endure in their localities. One challenge for partnerships including larger anchor institutions (regardless of sector) is to create ongoing lines of communication and cooperation with community residents. These partnerships benefit from established interface with liaisons to communities, especially the most underserved populations. In some instances, these liaisons are smaller nonprofit organizations.

They could be churches. As the COVID-19 pandemic enters a phase in which vaccines are available, one of the problems community partnerships must solve is how to reach lower-income, often communities of color, who are disconnected from many established resources or are even untrusting of hospitals and the existing health-care infrastructure. In some instances, churches are playing the role of liaisons to these communities. Instead of asking residents to leave their neighborhoods and visit anchor institutions such as hospitals or stadiums to receive a vaccine, a local church frequented by local residents could be an appropriate bridge. These are places residents might trust. They might feel more comfortable visiting their local church to receive a vaccine.

The international partnerships featured in this book tend to include various creative structures for liaising with lower-income communities. Chipatala Cha Pa Foni (CCPF) in Malawi and Parivartan in India both engage representatives of grassroots communities in order to raise health awareness with their peers, for example. If a community partnership seeks to solve problems at the community level that are most adversely affecting historically underserved constituents, it must develop bridges to directly interface with these populations. There is no single model in this regard, as demonstrated in the experiences of the partnerships in this book. But if the goal is genuinely to solve local problems, some systems should be instituted in order to ensure direct engagement at the grassroots level. In some instances, community partnerships become hubs for activity and sharing among institutions that, on their own, are more directly connecting with residents. The Newark Anchor Collaborative, for example, is a community of practice among anchor institutions, all of which have active programming in local communities. The partners come together to share ideas and lessons on their respective community partnerships to mutually strengthen their institutional efforts.

Many of the partnerships focusing on larger anchor institutions emphasize investment in local communities. They highlight local hiring and purchasing, for example. These partnerships tailor their ongoing investments to the community. They prioritize training and hiring local residents. They emphasize purchasing from local businesses or encourage contractors to hire locally. They may also highlight the need to address local infrastructure that affects the entire region in areas such as transportation. Overall, successful community partnerships are driven by the pursuit of a common good. They seek to solve problems that will enhance a given locality on many levels. Indeed, the partners have a vested interest in their locality, but community partnerships recognize both the opportunity to serve institutional interests and enhancing the well-being of those beyond their walls. This is an important dimension that distinguishes community partnerships from more transactional collaborations that are designed to achieve an end that essentially serves the partners.

Community partnerships are willing to grapple with complexities in community and economic development. One aspect of this complexity is an emphasis on people – the people who are currently residing in a community, especially those who are most underserved. Many development initiatives are focused on expanding the economy of a physical place regardless of outcomes for the existing population. These are the circumstances that often lead to displacement and gentrification in some contexts. In other contexts, this might mean simply a continuation of a status quo that benefits those who are already privileged and excludes those who are not. Another aspect is pure institutional self-interest – when institutions engage in collaboration to serve their ends without regard for broader potential community-wide benefits. Effective community partnerships continually reflect on how to maximize community benefit and emphasize equity. Some partnerships refer to "equitable development" or "equitable growth" in order to separate from approaches that do not transcend institutional self-interests or lead to gentrification.

Community partnerships must also grapple with the real nature of inequality in their communities. Therefore, they must directly address the full range of factors at work (e.g. racial inequity). Moving On Up in England is directly focusing on increasing employment among young Black men, for example. They have developed a highly specified approach, because the truth of data on employment tells them that this particular population requires specific attention. Therefore, they are not only targeting this population, they have organized their programming in a way that seeks to cater to the needs, interests, and realities of this population. The aforementioned approaches to liaising with constituents, in this instance, must be particular to young Black men. As community partnerships view their surroundings in the wake of the COVID-19 pandemic, they must also recognize how the public health and economic impacts of the pandemic differentially impacted various constituents. In many ways, the pandemic exacerbated existing racial and gender inequities in many communities, for example. Community partnerships must take an honest assessment of the realities around them, and adapt their programming accordingly.

## Sustainable, Long-Term Commitment and Program Development

Along the lines of viewing the post pandemic future, successful community partnerships seek to create lasting impact. Even in the case of El Salado, which is no longer in existence in Colombia, the partnership sought to fully transform a traumatized and devastated community. It ultimately altered the entire way in which community residents live and engage in governance and decision making. This is an example of a partnership that did not merely alter data points in some key social indicators. They built the capacity of the community, from the grassroots level, to democratically and collectively self-govern. This is a transcendent level of impact, which illustrates the potential of community partnerships to influence lasting change.

The notion of sustainability is an important component in community partnerships. In one sense, these formations are not easy to maintain. They are multifaceted with numerous partners representing different fields. But they have their locality in common. The collective belief in improving their surroundings keeps them together. But sustainability also means results – the kind of lasting impact they can influence. The nature of this change can be both external (throughout the community) and internal (inside of the institutions themselves). The Anchor Institutions Task Force refers to "mutually transformative partnerships" in which institutions participating in local collaborative pursuits are willing to change and evolve as they participate in partnerships. In making racial equity a signature program, the Newark Anchor Collaborative has created a forum through which its various member institutions seek to mutually improve how they combat systemic racism in their community as well as within their institutions. The internal and external are mutually reinforcing. An institution is better equipped to develop external programs seeking racial equity if the institution itself is intentionally becoming more racially equitable.

The Quality Jobs Fund (QJF) and the example of the Central Valley Fund are seeking to transform local economies for the long run. QJF is based on an evolving theory that providing an increasing number of underserved constituents access to high-quality jobs will improve the economic well-being of those individuals, their families, and their communities. This economic change will lead to an increased ability to purchase homes and build wealth. QJF also theorizes that the small and medium-sized businesses that hire new employees will benefit from stable workers, who will enhance their production and profitability. QJF hopes that these results will influence thinking in industries as well as in policy. This community partnership is driven by long-term prospects, hoping short-term investments will catalyze sustained repercussions leading to transforming economies.

Private philanthropy plays a central role in various aspects of sustaining partnerships and helping community partnerships' ability to stimulate long-term impact. Most of the partnerships in this book were created by private philanthropy. The lone outlier Metropolitan Partnerships in Australia is a governmental initiative. But it requires funding nonetheless. Sustained funding is crucial to community partnerships' survival, but partnerships are also challenged to become sufficient beyond philanthropy. Lasting change is embedded in some systems. Some partnerships seek to be embedded in government. Others, such as the Central Corridor Anchor Partnership in Minneapolis, have been self-sustaining their partnership. However lasting systems are forged, private philanthropy can be catalytic in establishing the path to sustainability. Successful community partnerships are intentional about how they will sustain their work. It becomes built into their overall approach and operations.

It is actually difficult to imagine a single foundation's funding supporting a community partnership's work for more than perhaps a decade. Moreover, locally based foundations, such as community foundations, are anchor institutions in themselves with a vested interest in strengthening their locality. The role they play in community partnerships transcends funding. As demonstrated in many examples of community partnerships, philanthropic institutions not only have the capacity to provide financial capital, they also have the ability to convene. They play an important role in helping to bring partners to the table and keeping them there over time.

### Alternative Forms of Governance and Influence

These partnerships have some freedom in functioning that allows them to create new approaches, often filling voids left by established systems. As is evident throughout the U.S., even though the established political system is democratic, many grassroots constituents at the community level have limited influence. New paths to influence must be created in civil society. This is a part of the basis of the nonprofit sector, which has the potential to amplify the voices of local residents. In the case of the Southeast Los Angeles Collaborative, private foundations and nonprofit organizations came together in order to strengthen the capacity of community-based nonprofit organizations and enhance the civic engagement of local constituents, who are primarily immigrants. They formed because of the disconnection of these residents from an ability to influence local policy.

Community partnerships can become alternative forms of governance. This is not an effort to replace government, but rather a new way to directly involve organizations and individuals in helping to shape the future of their communities. They can actually enhance the capacity of local government. Indeed, they can fill voids left by government, but they can also hold government accountable and advocate for policies that consider the lived experiences of local residents. With respect to larger anchor institutions in community partnerships, government can greatly benefit from aligning goals with local employers. The Memphis Medical District Collaborative can target the hiring and purchasing of various significant employers to the local economy. This is a direct benefit to local government. If residents of a municipality gain additional income through jobs and contracts, they bring additional taxes into local government. Community partnerships can complement the aims of local government, while remaining independent. Their independence leads to flexibility and creativity. Their thinking is not bound by established governmental bureaucracy. Funding from private foundations enables many community partnerships to engage in innovative and creative thinking to solve problems in localities.

Community partnerships also enable cross-sector collaboration and communication that probably should happen anyway, but often does not materialize automatically. Community partnerships become new structures through which new lines of communication across sectors are formed. These emerging connections lead to new ideas and solutions, including policy recommendations that can affect infrastructure, wages, transportation, safety, education, health, and any number of factors that shape the quality of life in a neighborhood, city, town, or region. The flexibility of community partnerships can also help them demonstrate what is possible through collaboration. They can launch pilot initiatives in which success is achieved on a particular concern, which ultimately influences policy. In the case of CCPF in Malawi, a health-care access initiative was piloted in a single district with the intent of nationalizing the program through the Malawi Ministry of Health. This is a case in which a cross-sector community partnership catalyzed by global philanthropy intentionally piloted a new initiative with government expecting to apply lessons from the approach into long-term policy change. In this context, external partners, without political restrictions or bureaucratic barriers, were able to help government develop new public health solutions.

Community partnerships, which are essentially nonprofit endeavors, can be opportunities for local governments. The nonprofit sector is so significant in community partnerships, not only because of its role as partner. Many community partnerships are nonprofit organizations in themselves. Community partnerships become entities, bringing new needs for staffing and coordination. In some instances, community partnerships create new nonprofits. In some others, they are housed in existing ones. This is significant regarding private philanthropy, as foundations need a nonprofit home for their funding. Nonprofit organizations can receive funds from foundations. This is a fairly standard model in the U.S. context. But, as previously indicated, this is not the case in many international contexts with relatively small nongovernmental sectors. However, international nongovernmental organizations can draw philanthropic funding from global foundations in order to support community partnerships on the ground in other countries, as illustrated in CCPF in Malawi and Parivartan in India. In both instances, the Bill and Melinda Gates Foundation brought philanthropic resources to external international contexts.

Community partnerships are also not bound by the approaches of any single sector. The strategic intent is to solve problems, and harness any range of ideas accordingly. They can leverage private-sector tactics for social ends, as is the case with the QJF. In this instance, a bank – the Federal Home Loan Bank of San Francisco – established an investment fund at a foundation – the New World Foundation. The New World Foundation, in turn, makes forgivable loans to intermediary organizations (nonprofit as well as for profit). These intermediary organizations are then charged with investing funds into small and medium-sized businesses in order to hire local constituents into jobs of significant quality. This is a relatively traditional private capital investment approach applied to enhance local economies. The goal is reminiscent of a nonprofit or governmental program. But the tactic is drawn from private banking. In this regard, community partnerships become vehicles for boundless creativity and innovation. Therefore, they can become vital tools for advancing societal and policy goals.

**Resources**

Community partnerships, as hubs of creativity and innovation, are poised to leverage expertise in various fields to collectively establish goals and solve problems. They can draw from a multitude of resources and sectors – one provides fiscal resources, another provides technical aspects of initiative development, another provides ongoing evaluation, etc. In some community partnerships, we can see leveraging of philanthropic assets, organizational assets, and business capabilities. Particularly in partnerships involving larger anchor institutions that are significant employers, strategies have led to business retention and expansion. They have driven inclusive and equitable economic growth, including creating new job opportunities for lower-income residents at anchor institutions. Many of these partnerships have built new strategic relationships between anchor institutions and local or small businesses for procurement opportunities.

Community partnerships can harness many other forms of resources. Indeed, they can bring in financial resources. Philanthropic resources can be fundamental, as noted. But they are not limited in terms of the number of philanthropic contributions or other forms of financial investment they can bring in. Moreover, one great strength of cross-sector collaboration is the wide range of different strategic insights that can emanate from partners in different fields. Those who are in health-related fields bring a particular form of expertise and perspective. This is also the case for those in education, banking, the arts, or any other field. This aggregation of thinking can lead to entirely new forms of knowledge and action.

An important consideration in community partnerships is how the resources of larger institutions can be leveraged to strengthen grassroots communities. One fundamental pathway to apply these resources is through enhancing the capacity of community-based nonprofit organizations. For example, in the case of the Southeast Los Angeles Collaborative, this has been the central goal of the partnership. Ideally, community partnerships strengthen civil society over the long run. These partnerships should stimulate a shift in the empowerment of constituents in local communities, especially those who are the least advantaged. Particularly in the U.S. context, community-based nonprofit organizations are the structures through which community voices are represented. This is not always the case, as unincorporated formations and small businesses play an important role as well in the local ecosystem at the grassroots level. In many international contexts, particularly in lower-income developing nations, the nonprofit sector is often not as present. But, some form of organization represents communities.

If community partnerships can harness resources across sectors and leverage philanthropy, anchor institutions, corporations, and other organizations possessing resources that can be of value to communities in order to strengthen the capacity of community-based nonprofits, they can enhance the voice and civic engagement of grassroots communities. These enhancements can bolster paths of communication and cooperation between grassroots constituents and larger institutions. They can also establish the foundation for community-driven public policy agendas.

As in the case of community partnerships and government, the potential impact is complementary. Community partnerships can complement government and lead to innovative forms of local government. Regarding community-based nonprofits, multi-institutional community partnerships can strengthen grassroots-level nonprofit organizations. They can funnel a breadth of resources to nonprofits, and directly impact communities. The range of contributions that community-based nonprofits bring to their localities is vast, from direct services to families and children to organizing residents for social change to fostering community development to influencing public policies, and beyond.

The different types of institutions participating in community partnerships (universities, hospitals, banks, etc.) can bring benefits as well. Communities can gain from the unique positions and influence of different partners to broaden local constituents' reach and access. These resources open new doors. For example, community residents might be able to use university research to support and bring credibility to issues of concern requiring further attention from policymakers. Institutions can provide data-driven research measurement reports – ongoing evaluation of programs and policies, identifying gaps, furthering campaigns or approaches. A few of the profiled partnerships have led to a better understanding of workforce metrics.

As stated, the value of philanthropic funding in community partnerships is substantial. These resources are flexible, and they provide partnerships support for the necessary work to create these new collaborative efforts. They support the planning and strategic thinking that allow partnerships to launch. Philanthropic resources can also help partnerships support the new budgetary items that emerge when they form. Partnerships ultimately create the need for staffing and other forms of organizational infrastructure, which require funding.

Ultimately, when community partnerships can truly transcend the public, private, and nonprofit sectors, they are poised to bring about comprehensive and the most adequate solutions to complex social and economic issues. Indeed, the kinds of issues facing local communities are effectively global – poverty, health, the environment, etc. But community partnerships are highly significant, because these issues are manifested in localities. The people who are confronted by challenges, such as the public health and economic concerns during the COVID-19 pandemic, experience these impediments in their homes, workplaces, neighborhoods, local institutions, and beyond. Successful community partnerships creatively harness a blend of resources, and apply them in pursuit of locally based solutions.

## Transcending Fields and Sectors

The power of community partnerships lies in their composition. These formations provide opportunities for institutions and leaders from different fields and sectors to come together and collectively work to improve their surroundings. With few opportunities to come together beyond fields and sectors, community partnerships provide unconventional spaces for mutual goal setting across traditional professional boundaries. Their collaborative journey together helps partners design strategies that recognize the complexity of and interdependence across their communities. Indeed, the multifaceted issues community partnerships are addressing are inherently not bound by a single sector. Housing, employment, health, and education are not single-sector issues. Moreover, they are all intertwined. Navigating these concerns is actually a cross-sector enterprise. In some ways, community partnerships are creating the kinds of varied teams necessary for a fuller understanding of the challenge that today's communities face.

The community partnerships profiled in this book are targeting multiple overlapping social issues simultaneously. At a more extreme level, a partnership such as El Salado focused on the comprehensive transformation of an entire municipality. Strategically, these comprehensive approaches are both focusing on particular complex issues, such as employment, as in the case of many of the profiled community partnerships. But they are doing so in recognition of the inextricable nature of the state of employment with the nature of the local economy with the quality of education, and beyond. The COVID-19 pandemic is such a striking tragedy confronting communities partly because of the ways in which it both highlighted and exacerbated an array of social impacts on the least advantaged segments of society. The lowest-income communities, particularly communities of color, faced the greatest health risks, and have been contracting and dying from the virus at higher rates. The most underserved populations continued to work in person at supermarkets, drug stores, public forms of transportation, and others in order to survive, yet remain at greater risk of exposure. Schools were teaching remotely, leaving those students without access to computers and the internet at even greater disadvantage. Some of these disadvantages were magnified by the quality of their housing. In order for community partnerships to solve pressing matters, especially those facing the populations that have been historically disenfranchised, they must recognize the interrelations among social and economic concerns. In the realities brought on by the pandemic alone, it is very apparent how various forms of resources and expertise housed in different fields and sectors can add value. Bridging medical, educational, financial, artistic, policymaking, cultural, and other forms of expertise leads to comprehensive solutions appropriate to the reality of needs.

Ultimately, community partnerships are challenged to contribute to enhanced quality of life for as many constituents as possible in their localities. Because of deep disparities and inequities, it seems logical that community partnerships should focus on those constituents that have born the brunt of adversity in their lives. In the case of the QJF, as well as in that of a few other partnerships, the creation of high-quality jobs is a pathway with comprehensive potential. This is an example of a partnership that is applying a narrow approach with a wide lens. Their strategic approach is based on an evolving theory of change that a quality job can have a significant impact on quality of life for not only an individual, but a family and a community. The approach projects repercussions that will transform an employee's ability to gain greater access, as a result of improved economic status, to food and nutrition, higher-quality health care, better housing, improved educational opportunities for children, and so on. A cross-sector community partnership is better able to envision this multiplier effect, but also to continually attend to it and identify what additional interventions are required in order to ensure a more comprehensive impact beyond a single job. Additional resources and partners, representing multiple fields, help fill gaps and expand the capacity of community partnerships to respond to local challenges comprehensively.

The breadth of fields represented in partnerships can bring additional benefits. For community-based nonprofit organizations, greater connections to the leadership of larger anchor institutions can enhance visibility and also improve the wider credibility of their work. Furthermore, the idea of collaboration among foundations, universities, corporations, and hospitals is one level of organization in communities. But collaboration across grassroots-level non-profit organizations is not guaranteed either, even in the same neighborhoods. In order for grassroots constituents to best benefit from collaboration with larger institutions, it is useful to create or strengthen community-based collaboration among smaller organizations. These formations can bolster the voice of constituents interfacing with larger organizations and local government. Ideally, community partnerships are contributing to a spirit of collaboration in local communities at every level of society. Grassroots collaboration among smaller organizations creates formations that more accurately represent the interests of underserved populations. This is an additional level of liaising with larger institutions in community partnerships.

## CHALLENGES

Beyond the various ways in which community partnerships are and can be successful, it is important to note the many challenges they face. These are complex arrangements that don't necessarily reflect a pre-existing culture of collaboration. As noted, professionals are accustomed to working within their fields. Their fields possess a particular style or custom of operating. The very act of convening partners and bringing them to the same table to engage in a discussion about their collective effort is a challenge. Once a community partnership is formed, it must develop a strategy and create programming. This programming focuses on complex issues that will not be solved quickly. Therefore, the challenge of time must always be acknowledged as we hope to understand the promise and potential pitfalls of community partnerships. At every stage of development, these formations must take realistic time horizons into account.

One aspect of time consumption in the process of developing partnerships is building commitment and trust. This is manifested on a number of levels. One significant way in which trust building emerges is through the barriers between grassroots constituents in communities and larger anchor institutions. Here again, the COVID-19 vaccination process comes to mind. Health-care institutions may offer the vaccine. The vaccine may be offered at universities, in stadiums, at performing arts centers, and other anchor institutions, but particular communities, especially communities of color, may be hesitant and untrusting. This same level of hesitation and mistrust surfaces through community partnerships' efforts to engage. Additionally, corporations or anchor institutions might not be fully committed themselves to fully engaging or including grass-roots constituents or community-based nonprofits. This is an ongoing matter facing community partnerships. Structurally, community partnerships seek to include various partner institutions. But functionally, they can represent only so many institutions and constituents. Therefore, they must figure out the best possible ways to continually liaise with and represent constituents. This is another way in which organized grassroots constituents and community-based organizations can maximize outcomes through direct lines of communication with institutionally based community partnerships.

Institutions do not necessarily know how to engage with communities. In some community partnerships, the participating institutions bring a breadth of history through their own community engagement programming. But many other institutions do not have a significant history of being engaged. They may even have tended to avoid engagement, as they may fear raising expectations. We must also acknowledge that many anchor institutions do not have a healthy relationship with their surrounding communities. Local communities may in fact perceive anchor institutions as part of the problem rather than the solution. When communities have historically been devastated by racism, poverty, and various inequities, they may not be particularly welcoming or hopeful. There is no true ending to the process of continuous engagement and trust building. For community partnerships, this must be treated as continuous work.

One other reason the very creation of a multi-institutional community partnership might be a significant achievement in itself is differing priorities among institutions. Community partnerships are transcendent because they galvanize various stakeholders around a common good. They bring institutions with different priorities and agendas to the table. These do not go away. Each institutional participant in a partnership must continually justify contin-ued involvement in a partnership. Therefore, community partnerships must constantly highlight and demonstrate interdependence. Indeed, institutional partnerships mutually benefit from their collective efforts. Community part-nerships must balance meeting institutional interests and addressing the needs of the most underserved constituents in their localities. They must achieve harmony across numerous interests that on one level compete but on another converge. Strategically, community partnerships' programming must simul-taneously serve various needs and interests. But there must be a cross-cutting purpose that fully connects. The Newark Anchor Collaborative views itself as a "community of practice."

The various anchor institutions participating in the partnership are continu-ally sharing and learning from each other and building a sense of community among institutions through this approach. It is based on peer learning on how each institution can best contribute to the community. It amplifies the existing efforts of the members. This degree of exchange also enables honest communication through which conflicts of interest among the institutions can actually be discussed. The institutions are each working to enhance local hiring and purchasing. They are also being encouraged to provide incentives for their employees to live in the city of Newark. The Newark Anchor Collaborative is also focusing on racial equity, recognizing a major challenge facing the general population in the city, and mutually building the capacity of each anchor institution to confront systemic racism externally in their community as well as strive to be more racially equitable internally. This is expanding the ability of each of these institutions to more authentically engage grassroots constituents in the city, and target their efforts to combat the many manifestations of systemic racism in all facets of life, as it shapes the existence of the city's Black and Latinx residents. This is one example of how a community partnership has constructed its strategic program design to help institutional partners endeavor toward shared interests among themselves and with Newark's population. They also intentionally aligned their employment goals with the City of Newark's, demonstrating an intentional effort to coordinate priorities with local government.

Another challenge for community partnerships is to be able to make a vision a reality in programming. As a number of the anchor institution-based partnerships in particular pursue employment goals, for example, there is much to consider. Once a partnership establishes a goal of increasing local employment, numerous questions must be answered. What kinds of jobs are local employers offering? What is the nature of these jobs? Do they offer career advancement opportunities? Additionally, many other questions arise regarding the local population and available jobs. Do the available jobs match the qualifications of the intended beneficiary population? For example, when the goal is to increase employment for lower-income populations with limited formal training or employment experience, the available jobs would have to be entry level. These may not be the vacant positions at local employers.

Matching prospective employees with available jobs at local employers could require new programming and staffing. It might also require additional layers of collaboration. Local residents might need additional training and education in order to be positioned to succeed in available jobs. Many community partnerships with local employment and procurement goals are not only seeking to place residents in jobs. Ultimately, their vision is to transform local economies and transition underserved populations out of poverty. Community partnerships should establish goals with a full understanding of what it will actually take to achieve them. Moving On Up in England is confronting a breadth of context that shapes employment realities. They are focused specifically on Black men. In order to create employment opportunities for this population, they must not only understand the mechanics of employers, jobs, and training. They must directly address systemic racism and connect with Black men with a broader understanding of their lived experiences.

The challenge of achieving program goals is also a matter of capacity. Intermediary nongovernmental organizations or community-based nonprofits may not have the capacity to take on new programming to help community partnerships meet their goals. Moreover, large institutional partners may not have the staffing or infrastructure to pursue new lines of work that are a departure from their typical procedures and operations. This reinforces the importance of hub organizations that embody partnerships as well as philanthropy to help support the staffing and administrative needs that come along with new programming. This also underscores the significance of community-based nonprofits that are already connected to local constituents and possibly experienced working on the programming partnerships hope to implement. All community partnerships are challenged to construct program goals that are ambitious yet realistic.

The COVID-19 pandemic has magnified this set of circumstances. The pandemic has not only decimated communities in the short term, it has created longer-term uncertainty. It is more difficult to plan and envision when it is hard to imagine the near future. Community partnerships have been responding to an immediate crisis, but there is less clarity about levels of capacity for sustainable responses over time. The pandemic has demonstrated to partnerships (and everyone) the value of flexibility or adaptive capacity. The pandemic forced partnerships to shift gears. Beyond the pandemic, flexibility is an important capability for community partnerships in general. Given the difficulty of achieving an ambitious set of goals in complex situations, it is important to plan for change. The notion of change should be considered a constant. During the several months spanning the pandemic, predictions about the spread of the virus have come and gone. The dominance of COVID-19 as a life-altering reality has persisted, challenging community partnerships to plan and adapt, and continue to do the same. Their efforts to contribute to lessening the impact of the pandemic on their localities has been spanning various phases from the initial responses to helping people maintain he vaccination period.

In the U.S., the federal government has been intervening with periodic relief packages, providing funds for individuals and families and support for small businesses. It has been purchasing vaccines to be distributed to states that in turn send vaccines to communities. But once the pandemic is over, the effects will remain. Students are behind in their schooling. Many more are unemployed or impoverished. Community partnerships will be challenged to do more in the face of an altered context.

# 18. Future opportunities, considerations, and directions

This context brings us to future opportunities for community partnerships. Between the pandemic's exacerbation of existing inequities and the increasingly apparent impacts of climate change, much more will be expected of community partnerships. In fact, much more will be expected of the nonprofit sector, philanthropy, and government in particular. Leadership has always played an important role in community partnerships, especially because these formations require intentional effort. They don't naturally emerge. They are unconventional. The leadership of philanthropy has played a crucial role in the development of most of the community partnerships profiled herein. Philanthropy brings the flexibility and resources for innovative thinking. This kind of thinking will be quite significant into the future, as we will be challenged to consider what it will take to actually solve pressing social problems.

This may be daunting, but this more urgent context is an opportunity to engage all elements of society in collaborative efforts. Government alone can accomplish only so much. The crises of our times certainly reaffirm the importance of strong and healthy government. It is important not to lose sight of this reality. Community partnerships that transcend sectors should complement government around shared priorities in public health, education, economic opportunities, and many other matters that are manifested at the local level. Leaders in all industries will have to advocate within their institutions in order to encourage their participation in pursuit of a common good beyond their singular organization interests. The reality of leadership in community partnerships is that leaders of participating institutions play an essential role. They approve their institution's involvement in partnerships, and must continue to reinforce their commitment to being engaged in partnerships internally. Leaders of universities, hospitals, foundations, corporations, and other institutions do not automatically see the need to join community partnerships. They may have to be persuaded. But leaders that are committed to community partnerships are valuable change agents. Stability among committed leaders will be necessary for the overall success of community partnerships in the future.

Leadership is also quite significant at the grassroots community level in which nonprofit organizations play an important role. In the quest to create authentic and inclusive collaboration between larger institutions and community residents, community-based organizations are in the position of channeling the voices and interests of local constituents. Leadership of community-based organizations is a vital component of the kind of capacity representative nonprofits need in order to maximize the value of community partnerships that involve larger institutions. As relationships in these arrangements help drive the work of these collaborations, consistency among leaders can bring great value. But organizations must avoid dependency on singular leaders. Community partnerships can be constructed to include various levels of leadership beyond chief executives.

Overall, community partnerships enable numerous advantages for institutions and residents. For institutions, community partnerships provide new ways to demonstrate relevance. Whatever the mission of the institution, community partnerships create new activities that can influence the way institutions operate. With external engagement through community partnerships, institutions can enhance their external communications and investment strategies. This also brings about greater exposure and visibility as well as new relationships across sectors. The same can be true for community-based nonprofit organizations, which possibly open avenues for additional streams of revenue through financial contributions from new sources. Connection to these partnerships could help community-based organizations expand their programs and initiatives and reach a greater number of community residents.

For community residents, these partnerships can bring many opportunities, particularly if they are able to achieve specific goals. They can lead to greater employment for residents. They can help grow local small businesses, which could be led by women or people of color, and hire from the community as they expand. As community partnerships can shine a light on local problems that are not receiving adequate attention, they can also influence local policy and infrastructure. In general, they can bring about greater equity and inclusion throughout local communities with the right approach. But, the opportunity of community partnerships is not only in the quantitative results they might be able to bring about in employment, health, education, or other issues. It is also in their capacity to alter the role in which institutions and communities as a whole engage and influence their local environments. They are new and extended forms of democratic engagement that amplify and empower local constituents.

## ADDITIONAL CONSIDERATIONS

### Values

If community partnerships are to be valuable tools for solving pressing problems in localities and transforming communities, they must engage the most underserved populations. Additionally, institutions involved in these partnerships, whatever their size, should be willing to adapt and change as a result of their participation in community partnerships. In other words, a university in a community partnership is not merely a source of expertise to be delivered to local residents, it should also be willing to learn from the community and consider how to adapt and evolve. Community partnerships can be structured in ways that do not benefit underserved populations. Partnerships involving larger anchor institutions, for example, sometimes lead to community and economic development that leads to circumstances such as gentrification.

Even with good intentions, market forces can sometimes create unintended consequences. But intentions matter, and community partnerships should be willing to continually self-examine and commit to a set of principles and values. The Anchor Institutions Task Force (AITF) has been promoting a values-based approach to the role of anchor institutions in community partnerships. The AITF's values include a commitment to place, collaboration, democracy and democratic practice, and social justice and equity.

**Strategic Role Playing**

What is apparent in observing community partnerships is that strategy is both design and action – structurally and programmatically. In the content of their work, community partnerships make strategic decisions about their programs and initiatives. They have many options they can pursue. Some partnerships come together for a specific purpose, such as health awareness about a particular disease. Many other community partnerships are not focused on a single issue. They are comprehensive in their approach because the overall quality of life in a specific locality is the essence of the goal.

The composition of a partnership is a factor in determining its agenda. In one sense, partnerships are intentional at the outset, deliberately identifying partners that can help achieve certain goals. For example, if the general desire is to enhance the local economy and ensure more jobs for local residents, then the partnership will want to include significant employers. In other instances, the partners required to achieve certain ends might not actually have a presence in the locality. Given these circumstances, partnerships have to be creative in order to identify resources from elsewhere, as is often the case in lower-income nations or in relatively resource-poor rural areas. In order to be effective, community partnerships require a number of roles to be fulfilled. It is useful to capture these categories.

## Partnership Roles

### Hub

A hub is a central organizing unit for a partnership. As noted, this role is often played by a nonprofit organization regardless of the fields represented by partners. In some instances, a hub entity is an existing organization. Sometimes it is a new organization created in order to embody the partnership. This hub is ultimately the functioning agent of a partnership that houses staff. It is also the home for the partnership's resources. If the partnership receives foundation grants, for example, the hub receives and manages these funds.

### Initial convener

Ultimately, some person or organization identifies the need for a community partnership, and decides to engage others about the prospects for a new collaborative body. This could be a foundation, a government agency, a nonprofit organization, or any other concerned institution or individual. As noted, foundations can be useful initial conveners because they may appear to be neutral, yet they are viewed as reputable enough to be able to bring various institutions together. Some of this ability to convene depends on the partners. For example, if the intent is to start a conversation with corporate chief executive officers, the convener would have to be an entity to whom they would respond. Strategically, the initial convener could make all of the difference in a partnership's ability to launch.

### Financer

Someone has to cover the cost of the partnership's work. In some cases, the partners might collectively chip in and cover the cost. But, in many cases, the funds for these partnerships come from other sources, such as foundations. As noted, the challenge for sustaining partnerships is to ensure that costs will be covered continually, well beyond the initial resources provided in order to launch a partnership. A community partnership cannot succeed if the partners are only willing to work together if an external source such as a foundation covers costs. Additionally, all funding is not the same. Some funding comes with significant restrictions, which could actually influence the nature of the partnership's work, and take their efforts in unintended directions. Partnerships should strive for as much autonomy as possible in their financing, as this very well may define programmatic strategy. Financing not only shapes the scale of a partnership's endeavors, it can define the content of this work.

### Community bridge (to grassroots, to government, to other fields)

As constructed, community partnerships are both inclusive and limited. They can never include every relevant constituent in a community at the table.

Therefore, they need community bridges or liaisons to particular constituents. These could be peers representing particular populations. Some of the partnerships in this book created bridges to grassroots constituents, who are the intended beneficiaries of the partnership's programming. Partnerships may require bridges to government or particular fields. As localities are ecosystems of various types of organizations and demographic groups, partnerships should strive to be as diverse as possible.

## Partnership catalyst

A partnership catalyst helps a partnership transition from idea to reality. This is often the role of an outside advisor or consultant – a role which I have played personally on various occasions. This is a role that includes helping a partnership assess its potential, identify partners, develop a strategic plan, and help design structure, programming, and finances.

## Learning partner

Another role I and my company, Marga Incorporated, have played is as a learning partner – an ongoing observer and participant monitoring progress and connecting partnerships to relevant resources from elsewhere. Some might see this as the role of an evaluator. But *learning* more accurately captures the breadth of knowledge deriving not only from the partnership's experiences, but from identifying additional resources in other communities, and actively learning with the partnership, thus the need to combine *learning* and *partner*. Marga is playing this role with both the Newark Anchor Collaborative and the Quality Jobs Fund.

## Resources and experts

Some of the community partnerships in this book include the institutions that have the resources the partnership intends to leverage on the community's behalf. For example, jobs and contracts are concrete resources required for local economic development. Matching these resources with the most underserved populations helps establish a greater degree of economic equity in the community. The participants in partnerships can bring a wide variety of other resources, such as expertise in particular fields (e.g. health care) that can be applied to solving local problems. In communities, resources are all around. All institutions and people at all levels have some form of expertise and value to share. The lowest-income communities have expertise to share on their experiences that shape our understanding of what it really requires to strengthen communities. Communities are rich with assets. The challenge for partnerships is to both build on existing assets and fill important voids. Some communities have the benefit of housing the assets that can address deficits. In these instances, partnerships are bridging a disconnection in the distribution of resources. This is the case in most of the U.S.-based partnerships in this book as well as Moving On Up in England. But in many contexts, the resources that are sorely needed are not in close proximity. As noted, these are instances where partnerships must make a resource leap, and work outside partners and funders.

# CREATING COMMUNITY PARTNERSHIPS

The AITF recognized that while many active community partnerships are strengthening their neighborhoods, cities, towns, and regions, many more could be created. If community partnerships are effective problem-solving mechanisms, then new community partnerships could be applied to address many other intractable challenges. Consequently, AITF created a new concept, Local Strategic Dialogues. These are targeted interventions designed to create new collaborative initiatives to solve a particular problem in a locality or region. This approach was tested in San Diego, California in the U.S. The University of San Diego agreed to serve as a host. We asked the university's president, James Harris, to identify a local problem that requires greater collaboration among various stakeholders across sectors to solve. Affordable housing was the chosen issue. Affordable housing is a significant issue, particularly in coastal urban areas in California. San Diego has actually been more affordable than other major metropolitan areas in the state, such as the San Francisco Bay Area.

As conversations evolved, the nature of the challenge at hand became increasingly focused, emphasizing moderate income housing as a particular problem. This is an issue that affects individuals in civil society, but also employers. Many of the employees at anchor institutions in the area would be categorized as moderate income. If they have difficulty finding sufficient housing, employers are presented with an obstacle. Once the problem was identified, we asked President Harris, "Who would be required in order to adequately increase the availability of moderate-income housing locally?" The Local Strategic Dialogues model relies on conversations with relatively small groups of stakeholders (up to 25 persons) to launch unprecedented action. The University of San Diego identified and invited housing advocates, real estate developers, local government officials, other major local employers, and housing researchers. A dialogue among this mix of stakeholders, in 2019, led to a new, focused strategy on "the missing middle" in order to ultimately lead to an expansion in moderate-income housing.

The inspiration for the Local Strategic Dialogues model was an ongoing partnership between AITF and the Council of Europe. Through communication about the role of institutions of higher education in their communities, the Council of Europe expressed an interest in creating a network similar to AITF across Europe, focused particularly on the local mission of higher education. AITF facilitated a series of conversations along with the council, which brought together various representatives of particular universities and higher education associations across Europe on bringing greater attention to the role that universities can play in democratic community partnerships. The method of convening relevant stakeholders in order to create new partnerships, applied on a continental level, seemed to have potential value in localities. As a result, AITF began crafting a model for Local Strategic Dialogues that led to a pilot launching in San Diego.

Now the challenge is to consider how to catalyze the development of new partnerships where necessary at a greater scale. At this moment, local communities around the world are grappling with a public health and economic crisis, and will be faced with the aftermath. How can community partnerships help localities handle the challenges ahead? We will need to harness existing partnerships, as some of the partnerships featured herein have done during the pandemic. But we will also have to assess circumstances and create new partnerships, as the Local Strategic Dialogues model is designed to address.

Overall, community partnerships are important vehicles for strengthening localities. They are pathways to solving problems in health, housing, education, employment, and beyond. But they are so much more than the potential results they can influence. They are creative forms of participation and democratic governance that can complement the public sector and provide meaningful roles for various people and institutions in a geographic area. Their impact can be localized, but the learning that we can gain from each community partnership's experiences can bring many lessons to how communities in various parts of the world in different types of environments can organize themselves. The role of philanthropy and the nonprofit sector in these partnerships is tremendous. The impact of a foundation's grant to help start a community partnership can be a multiplier effect. It can not only bridge necessary coordination and communication among institutions that might not otherwise collaborate, but it can also foster lasting change. The nonprofit sector, in its vastness from grassroots nonprofits to large anchor institutions, finds expanded relevance in community partnerships. These partnerships amplify work already underway. As nonprofits maintain specific social missions, they have an opportunity to impact society at new levels through community partnerships.

Community partnerships can also maximize corporate social missions, wielding potential well beyond any single corporation's community relations. Additionally, the work of local governments is significantly complemented by these formations that are ultimately laboring toward public ends. They are created channels through which the private and nonprofit sectors can leverage their resources and expertise to enhance the quality of life in localities. Envisioning the many challenges that could surface in the coming years, it is hard to imagine that community partnerships will not play a substantial role. The COVID-19 pandemic and natural disasters provide clues into the nature of potential future crises and also underscore why community partnerships are so important. Certainly, we will need cross-sector collaboration and coordination globally. But the great issues of our times will be experienced at home. They must be solved accordingly.

It is not surprising that many of the community partnerships featured in this have been active in combatting the pandemic in their communities. At every phase, from the emergence of the virus to the distribution of vaccines, community-based coordination and collaboration across sectors have been required. The strategies to address and solve the next pandemic, the next weather emergency, or the next economic crisis will require community partnerships. For this reason, these formations must be taken much more seriously. They should be more well known, better understood, and more significantly financed. They should also be considered fundamental in policymaking, as they are truly the kinds of tools that government should consider in order to navigate the very complex times ahead.

## DIRECTIONS

Ultimately, community partnerships will be required in order to navigate and solve the most pressing matters of our times, as people will experience public health crises, natural disasters exacerbated by climate change, economic instability, limited access to affordable housing or education, aging infrastructure, and a variety of other challenges – in their neighborhoods, cities, towns, and regions. This is not to suggest that we do not also need global cooperation across borders. Something of the magnitude of the Paris Climate Accord, for example, is essential to solving the climate crisis, bringing multiple nations together to coordinate. None of the most vexing challenges are merely contained in place. But local action must simultaneously accompany collaboration and coordination across nations and sectors globally. At every level, some form of strategic partnership is vital to the future.

Nevertheless, at the community level, local governments, philanthropic institutions, nonprofit organizations, and other institutions have much to consider about the role they can play as engaged local actors. This is relevant across sectors and industries.

### Philanthropy

The role of philanthropy in community partnerships has been illustrated in the experiences of the featured community partnerships. As philanthropy continues to expand around the world, it must continue to evaluate its role in communities. Philanthropic institutions can bring partners together and help create community partnerships. Foundations must consider how to identify potential partners and engage in a respectful manner. While philanthropy can bring people together, it can also drive the agenda.[1] Philanthropy must reflect on the right balance between being a convener and a catalyst and a funder while also being a true partner. How can philanthropic institutions and philanthropists add value to local communities while allowing communities to define an agenda? How can foundations remain open to *community-driven philanthropy*?[2]

Foundations that support community partnerships must also address the role of their funding in community partnerships. Indeed, this kind of flexible support enables many community partnerships to form. But community partnerships take time to develop. Foundations in community partnerships are challenged to provide long-term support over several years, but also help identify other sources of support. In many ways, community partnerships fulfil the need of many foundations to broaden and extend impact. One grant for a single project can accomplish only so much, but support to facilitate the creation of collaboration that leverages resources from multiple sectors is definitively more of a long-term agenda. Simultaneously, community partnerships should take on a life of their own, and seek to become self-sustaining. Obviously, some partners are better positioned than others to financially contribute. A part of a foundation's role is to help community partnerships think creatively about their financial sustainability over time.

## Community-Based Nonprofits

This book features a wide range of nonprofit organizations from large hospitals that are substantial local employers to grassroots organizations. As in other sectors, levels of resources vary across institutions. Grassroots community-based nonprofit organizations play a particular role, as they are representative of, often underserved, constituent populations, who may lack access and influence in their localities. These organizations, therefore, become a representative voice. But there is no guarantee that a community-based nonprofit organization is representative of the community it serves. Community partnerships, as noted, truly require liaisons to local communities in order to be truly effective. Community-based nonprofit organizations, therefore, must continually challenge themselves to be as connected as possible to constituents.

Local communities include networks of organizations. At the grassroots level, community-based nonprofits coexist with small businesses and unincorporated associations. How can community-based organizations play a role in coordinating neighborhood-level participation in order to interact with community partnerships that may include larger organizations? In processes such as the development of Community Benefits Agreements, some coordinated entity must represent communities in engaging a large physical development project, for example. How can the nonprofit sector embody civil society and become a pathway toward greater voice and influence among the most underserved populations? Due to competing interests, such as competition for funding, many nonprofit organizations are not collaborating, sometimes in the same neighborhood. This is a challenging barrier to ensuring that constituent voices are positioned to negotiate with larger institutions from a position of strength.

## Nonprofit Anchor Institutions

Clearly, anchor institutions are playing a significant role in community partnerships. While anchor institutions come in various sizes, large employers, as anchors in their communities, can wield significant influence, and bring substantial resources, such as jobs. The anchor institutions of decades ago were often large corporations in fields such as manufacturing and retail. Particularly in developed nations, the anchor institutions of today are among the most significant local employers, as large nonprofit organizations such as hospitals and universities. These various types of nonprofit anchors are facing various considerations in relation to community partnerships.

## Institutions of Higher Education

Colleges and universities bring a breadth of assets to their communities. Not only are they corporate entities with land, jobs, and contracts, they are also hubs of knowledge across numerous fields. They have students and faculty who can deploy knowledge on behalf of communities. Although they bring knowledge, institutions of higher education must respect community-based knowledge, and be willing to learn. In community partnerships, colleges and universities should be willing to participate in mutually transformative partnerships in which the institution plays a role in strengthening the community while being willing to change itself.

But, overall, institutions of higher education are driven by a knowledge mission. They encourage and produce knowledge through teaching, service, and learning for the betterment of society. Community partnerships provide universities and colleges an opportunity to apply their mission to solving local problems. Institutions of higher education can extend their local impact by combining resources with others in their localities. Higher education as a field is undergoing significant changes, as the industry is evolving and adapting in changing times. Through community engagement, institutions of higher education demonstrate their relevance. They have an opportunity to apply their mission in their own surroundings.

## Health Institutions and Systems

Hospitals and health systems are also mission-driven. In many communities, they are now the largest employers. The pandemic has placed them in a spotlight like at no other time in modern history. Their value to society is undeniable. Through community partnerships, health anchor institutions can contribute to community health not only clinically. Given the significance of the social determinants of health in defining health outcomes, health anchors can contribute to health and well-being through expanding employment and educational opportunities or increasing units of affordable housing or improving air quality. Disparities in communities are influenced by *equity factors*. We can look at a single issue such as health outcomes, but with the understanding that a person's health is impacted by one's wealth, influence, access, exposure, and more. Communities, in many ways, are microcosms of society. They include a breadth of intersecting issues that determine all aspects of a person's quality of life.

Health institutions' engagement in community partnerships in order to solve any range of issues ultimately comes back to community health. The degree to which hospitals can extend their impact on health through collaboration with other institutions across fields and sectors is, in itself, an extension of their mission. This is a mutually beneficial reality. Engagement in community partnerships makes quite a bit of sense for health institutions. Because they bring such significant resources as purveyors of health services as well as economic engines, they can contribute to solving crucial concerns facing communities. Moreover, the health industry continues to grow, along with tremendous societal needs. It needs a workforce to meet these needs. As illustrated in a few of the featured community partnerships, hospital-based jobs strategies can be quite mutually beneficial. Jobs in health can potentially provide low-income communities not only employment, but career opportunities.

## Cultural Anchors

While cultural anchors often do not employ to the extent of hospitals, they play an important role in communities that is worth noting. They can carry the culture, distinctiveness, and history of communities. They can provide avenues for creative expression. As communities emerge from the pandemic, the need for artistic expression will be significant. The arts industry has been particularly devastated by the pandemic due to the limitation of in-person activities. In a city such as New York, the arts represent an economic engine, as they drive tourism, and bring a constant flow of capital into the city. In community partnerships, cultural anchors such as museums and performing arts centers will be positioned to bring people together. They will also be positioned to help communities navigate difficult conversations. Through expression, the arts can address challenging issues, such as racial tension and inequity in unique ways.

## Private Corporations

For private corporations, community partnerships can bring many opportunities as well. In some instances, private corporations overlap with private philanthropy. Therefore, they face similar considerations as foundations. But they also are confronted by their interdependence with their localities. Many of today's private corporations are not considered as anchor institutions because of their ability to leave. They might decide a location is not worth their while, and seek lower operating costs somewhere else. They might seek tax breaks from local governments in order to remain in their current location. Community partnerships can ground private corporations in their localities. As noted, being an anchor institution is not only an objective reality, it is also a subjective matter of choice. A corporation can choose to be committed to place. If the place in which a corporation is located is more equitable and functioning effectively, the corporation benefits. Its employees benefit as well. Certainly, private corporations span the universe of types of industries, so the nature of their engagement partly depends on their field. Some corporations, for example, rely on a local customer base. They may have a clearer vested interest in being locally engaged than some others. The shift to remote work that has been accelerated by the pandemic could have a significant impact on how corporations perceive their interest in their locality.

## Government

At the local level, community partnerships have the opportunity to extend the impact and influence of government, as demonstrated in the experiences of many of the featured community partnerships. Community partnerships can essentially be of assistance to local government. They can produce jobs for residents that can increase the local tax base. They can improve community health. They can lend space, as we have seen so prominently during the pandemic, as various anchor institutions served as testing and vaccination sites. The list of opportunities is lengthy. It is somewhat surprising that more local governments have not actively sought out collaboration with local universities or hospitals or other potential partners.

Strategically, local governments have more of a vested interest in catalyzing the development of community partnerships than private philanthropy.

Without speculating too much, government is political and bureaucratic. These dynamics may create barriers to local government's active outreach to nongovernmental partners. Moreover, these dynamics have different consequences in countries with limited philanthropy, and a small nongovernmental sector. The political dimension of government at all levels is more apparent in highly partisan contexts. This can lead to a lack of trust among various constituents, limiting a government's ability to be perceived as a somewhat neutral convener. A community foundation might be viewed differently. Additionally, leadership turnover is a reality in all industries, but in government, it is built in. Mayors are on term limits. Regardless of changes at the top in government, there is stability underneath.

In the U.S., at the federal level, the leadership of government agencies changes, such as the Department of Labor or the Department of Education. But the bulk of the career staff remains in place. Many programs transcend the lives of various administrations regardless of party. Therefore, the AITF has been advocating for greater support for the role of anchor institutions in rebuilding and reimagining their communities in the federal government. This is with the assumption that a fund could become embedded in a federal agency that provides additional support for anchor institutions to be engaged in community partnerships. This is particularly needed among community-centric anchor institutions – entities that might not be as large or wealthy that directly serve the most underserved populations. SBH Health System in the Bronx, New York, for example, is a health anchor. But it serves one of the lowest-income populations in the U.S. As this largely poor, Black, and Latinx population was disproportionately contracting COVID-19, SBH was overwhelmed with patients – patients without private insurance. It is important to highlight the unique role that these community-centric anchor institutions can play in community partnerships.

## Community Partnerships

For existing community partnerships, there is much to consider in our extraordinary times. It is useful to explore the point of view of partnerships at different stages of development.

### Emerging

The emerging stages of a community partnership can be exhilarating. Once partners are convened, and in general agreement about goals and a strategy, there is a sense of accomplishment. But this formative period can be fraught with uncertainty. As indicated regarding the Local Strategic Dialogues framework of the AITF, identifying the most relevant partners to initially convene can be pivotal. If a small group initially decides to pursue creating a partnership, various questions about potential participants can surface. How many partners should be invited in the early stages? Should the partnership focus on the largest institutions primarily? How can institutional partners and the broader community interact in the resulting partnership?

The Local Strategic Dialogues model identifies a single issue first, and builds the partnership based on who would be essential to working on the issue. This is one approach to initial strategic design. Another approach is to focus on the institutions that are already actively engaged in the community, and view the partnership as a way in which the collaborating institutions can coordinate their efforts and eventually jointly create a program agenda. Another approach can be to bring together the institutions with the most substantial resources to try to detect their interest in harnessing their jobs, expertise, facilities, etc. for community benefit. However the partnership starts, ultimately, it will have to develop lines of communication with the broader population. This is where community-based nonprofit organizations can play an important role. An early-stage partnership could also attempt to align goals with a foundation (or group of foundations) or with local government. Ultimately, it would be wise to explore alignment with local government at some point in a community partnership's evolution.

Context matters significantly in determining an initial strategy. What is the history of collaboration among institutions toward a greater good locally? Do institutions work well together or tend to compete? What is the reputation of institutions in underserved communities? What are the local demographics and the state of racial inequities and poverty? What are the top three most pressing issues facing the locality? These kinds of questions should be fully explored at the early stages. In some communities, it is not a major departure for local institutions to be engaged. In others, this is far from the case. Across different nations, various dynamics regarding philanthropy and nonprofits come into play, as evidenced in the profiled partnerships in developing countries. If philanthropic resources are not present locally, how can the initial designers of a partnership identify sources of support? International giving by U.S. and European foundations has played an important role in helping partnerships launch.

Given how the pandemic has been decimating communities, it would not be a surprise to see many new multi-institutional community partnerships forming. It would not be shocking to see many leaders in various fields conclude that challenging social issues can only be solved by way of some form of collaboration. It is important for those hoping to create new partnerships to thoroughly assess the landscape of their community, the nature of local assets, and the potential for collaboration. Once a partnership forms, all of the factors any start-up organization would face come into play. What is an appropriate budget? What is the partnership's structure?

It is important for early-stage partnerships to gain the buy-in of institutional leaders. Because partnerships ask institutions to transcend their singular organizational priorities, engagement in the partnership has to be clearly justifiable for all of the institutional partners. The leaders of the institutions will have to be champions of the idea of participating in the partnership in order to remain involved. The programming[3] of emerging partnerships should be realistic. Perhaps they begin by working on a single issue or initiative, and expand over time. But it is useful to craft a longer-range vision for the partnership. If not a detailed strategic plan, then a frame of a plan should be created in order to engage participants in what it will take to achieve their goals. This level of dialogue forces discussion on sustaining the partnership, identifying the right partners, and managing expectations.

### Intermediate and advanced

Intermediate and advanced partnerships are already functioning with programming in place. Intermediate-stage community partnerships are likely beginning discussions about second or third strategic plans, seeking to keep partners energized. They are grappling with how they will finance and sustain their efforts over time. If a philanthropic partner has been covering costs, this institution might be encouraging the partnership to diversify sources of revenue. Most of the profiled partnerships are at the intermediate level. One (El Salado) worked its way out of existence. Its sustainability over time was driven by the vast buy-in among an array of partners and constituents in the local community. The partnership as an organizational entity ended, but the work it stimulated continues. It is embedded in the local community and local government, as it has changed local ways of operating and decision making. The Career and College Access Pathway partnership could be categorized as an advanced partnership, which is sustaining itself through its partners that are paying dues to the collaboration. An advanced community partnership is self-sustaining even if foundations are still participating and providing financial support. These partnerships are also concerned about their impact. They may have systematic evaluation or assessment methods in place, producing data. If a partnership is advanced, perhaps in existence for over a decade, having implemented programs and achieved impact, it is likely recording and disseminating its story. Perhaps it produces an annual report or distributes a newsletter providing progress reports.

As demonstrated in the profiled partnerships' experiences, the emergence of a crisis such as the COVID-19 pandemic tests a community partnership's relevance. It challenges a partnership's ability to coordinate and convene and deploy resources to meet pressing local needs. Going forward, intermediate and advanced community partnerships are likely discussing how they expand the capacity of their efforts. If they have employment initiatives, the challenge is greater, as the pandemic has placed millions more into poverty and caused widespread unemployment. The pandemic sprung many foundations and philanthropists into greater action.[4] The magnitude of the challenge facing communities sets the stage for existing community partnerships and increased philanthropic support in local communities to converge. It will be intriguing to see how new community partnerships form and existing ones evolve in the coming years.

## FINAL THOUGHTS

Finally, community partnerships should receive far greater attention as innovative forms of local governance that can be applied to both fill voids and create new solutions that would not exist without the combined resources and expertise across various fields and sectors. As these partnerships continue to evolve, they are faced with an increasingly complex and even daunting reality. Recent events have only exacerbated existing inequities, including those by race and gender. Community partnerships will have to approach disparities directly, and recognize the true nature of inequities. They will have to develop authentic and democratic relationships with the most underserved constituents and pursue equitable goals. Indeed, communities are comprised of interdependent ecosystems. Institutions have a stake in participating in community partnerships that can improve their entire localities. But the pursuit of self-interest by institutions does not automatically lead to equity in communities. Community partnerships are not always driven to transform their localities in a manner that benefits those that are most adversely impacted by the great challenges of our times. Overall, these collaborative endeavors are complicated and time consuming. To some, they may not appear to be worth the time and energy. But the experiences of the community partnerships profiled herein suggest that creative leveraging of resources across fields and sectors can solve problems, increase civic engagement, and extend the effectiveness and impact of government. The social missions of philanthropic institutions and nonprofit organizations bring to community partnerships the dedication to community change that can help prioritize a commitment to equitable community change. If communities are to strengthen and successfully emerge from crises of the magnitude of a global pandemic, then community partnerships will be necessary. If communities are to become more resilient and positioned to handle the crises of the future, community partnerships are necessary. If the goal is to reduce persistent disparities, community partnerships will be required. We have reached a pivotal global moment when we will have to be creative and transcend traditional boundaries. Community partnerships represent one avenue to the solutions of the future.

## NOTES

1.  This is an issue that I addressed in more depth in *Philanthropy and Society* (Maurrasse 2020).
2.  Dr. Colin Greer and I have been developing the notion of "community-driven philanthropy" which draws upon many emerging trends in the field, such as trust-based philanthropy and participatory grantmaking. This notion is more comprehensive. It is about the degree to which philanthropy allows itself to be more fully immersed as a community partner in itself.
3.  My earlier book on public–private partnerships, *Strategic Public Private Partnerships* (Maurrasse, 2013) explored the dynamics of developing partnerships and designing their structure and plan in greater detail.
4.  The U.S.-based nonprofit, Candid, has been tracking philanthropy's response to the pandemic.

# References

American Civil Liberties Union (2006b). Appeals Court ruling ends the criminalization of homelessness. *ACLU Press Releases*, April 14. Retrieved from www.aclu.org/press-releases/aclu-southern-california-wins-historic-victory-homeless-rights-case

Ashraf, N., Ahmadsimab, A., and Pinkse, J. (2017). From animosity to affinity: The interplay of competing logics and interdependence in cross-sector partnerships. *Journal of Management Study*, *54*(6), 793–822.

Bendell, J. (2011). *Evolving Partnerships*. London: Routledge.

Bivens and Shierholz. (2020). Despite some good provisions, the CARES Act has glaring flaws and falls short of fully protecting workers during the coronavirus crisis. Economic Policy Institute. Retrieved from: https://www.epi.org/blog/despite-some-good-provisions-the-cares-act-has-glaring-flaws-and-falls-short-of-fully-protecting-workers-during-the-coronavirus-crisis/

Business Executives' Research Committee (1959). *Economic Development of the Greater Newark Area: Recent Trends and Prospects*. New Brunswick, NJ: Rutgers University.

California Community Foundation (n.d.). 2018 annual report dedication. Retrieved from www.calfund.org/2018annualreport/dedication/

Cantor, N., Cooper, T., Brown, M., and Englot, P. (2019). Tackling "the two Americas" with city-wide collaboration in Newark. *Journal on Anchor Institutions and Communities*, *2*(1), 27–38.

Clarke, A. and MacDonald, A. (2016). Outcomes to partners in multi-stakeholder cross-sector partnerships: A resource-based view. *Business and Society*, *58*(2).

Community Wealth (2020). Initiative for a Competitive Inner City (ICIC). Retrieved from https://community-wealth.org/content/initiative-competitive-inner-city-icic

Council on Foundations (2021) Community Foudnations. Retrieved from: https://www.cof.org/foundation-type/community-foundations-taxonomy?navItemNumber=15626&page=5

Engler, M. and Engler, P. (2016). The massive immigrant-rights protects of 2006 are still changing politics. *Los Angeles Times*. Retrieved from www.latimes.com/opinion/op-ed/la-oe-0306-engler-immigration-protests-2006-20160306-story.html

Ferguson, L. and Zeuli, K. (n.d.). Newark's data-driven approach to leveraging its anchor assets. *Initiative for a Competitive Inner City*. Retrieved from https://icic.org/blog/newarks-data-driven/

Fisher-Bruns, D. and Logan-Robinson, N. (2018). Memphis Medical District Collaborative: Catalyzing change on a community level. Democracy Collaborative. Retrieved from https://democracycollaborative.org/sites/default/files/downloads/MMDC-web-smaller.pdf

Guarino, A. (2014). Time of despair, time of hope: New Jersey in the Great Depression. Garden State Legacy. Retrieved from https://gardenstatelegacy.com/files/Time_of_Despair_Time_of_Hope_Guarino_GSL24.pdf

Johnson. P.D. (2018). Global philanthropy report: Perspectives on the global foundation sector. *Harvard University's John F. Kennedy School of Government Report*.

Retrieved from https://cpl.hks.harvard.edu/files/cpl/files/global_philanthropy_report_final_april_2018.pdf

Koistinen, D. (2002). The causes of deindustrialization: The migration of the cotton textile industry from New England to the South. *Enterprise and Society, 3(*3), 484–485.

MacDonald, A., Clarke, A., Huang, L., Roseland, M., and Seitanidi M.M. (2018). Multi-stakeholder partnerships (SDG# 17) as a means of achieving sustainable communities and cities (SDG# 11). In Leah Filho, W. (ed.), *Handbook of Sustainability Science and Research* (pp. 193–209). Cham: Springer.

Martinez-Cosio, M. and Bussell, M.R. (2013). *Catalysts for Change: 21st Century Philanthropy and Community Development*. London: Routledge.

Maurrasse, D. (2013). *Strategic Public Private Partnerships*. Northampton, MA: Edward Elgar Publishing.

Maurrasse, D. (2018). From the MDGs to the SDGs: Cross-sector partnerships as avenues to development in the UN system. In Chon, M., Roffe, P., and Abdel-Latif, A. (eds), *Cambridge Handbook of Public-Private Partnerships, Intellectual Property Governance, and Sustainable Development Goals* (pp. 356–375). Cambridge: Cambridge University Press.

Maurrasse, D. (2020). *Philanthropy and Society*. London: Routledge.

Maurrasse, D. (2021). *Beyond the Campus: How Colleges and Universities Form Partnerships with Their Surrounding Communities*. London: Routledge.

Mendel, S.C. and Brudney, J.L. (2018). *Partnerships the Nonprofit Way: What Matters, What Doesn't*. Bloomington, IN: Indiana University Press.

Moran, M. (2014). *Private Foundations and Development Partnerships: American Philanthropy and Global Development Agendas*. London: Routledge.

National Center for Charitable Statistics, Urban Institute (2020). The nonprofit sector in brief. Retrieved from https://nccs.urban.org/publication/nonprofit-sector-brief-2019 #the-nonprofit-sector-in-brief-2019

National Council of Nonprofits (2019). Nonprofit impact matters: How America's charitable nonprofits strengthen communities and improve lives. Retrieved from www.no nprofitimpactmatters.org/?utm_source=web&utm_medium=site&utm_campaign= reports-page

Newark Alliance (2020a). Newark Anchor Collaborative (NAC). Retrieved from www .newark-alliance.org/programs/newarkAnchorCollaborative/

Newark Alliance (2020b). Our organization. Retrieved from www.newark-alliance.org

Newark Alliance (2021a). History of Newark Alliance. Retrieved from www.newark -alliance.org/about/our-history/

NewJerseyAlmanac.com (n.d.). History: The Great Depression and the 1930s. Retrieved from www.newjerseyalmanac.com/great-depression-and-1930s.html

Pierre, J. (ed.). (1998). *Partnerships in Urban Governance: European and American Experiences*. London: Palgrave Macmillan.

Pollock, M. J., Wennerstrom, A., True, G., Everett, A., Sugarman, O., Haywood, C., ... & Springgate, B. (2019). Preparedness and Community Resilience in Disaster-prone areas: Cross-sectoral collaborations in South Louisiana, 2018. American journal of public health, 109(S4), S309-S315

Pribbenow, P. and Beeth, L. (2019). Central corridor anchor partnership: Securing regional prosperity. *Journal on Anchor Institutions and Communities, 2*(1), 54–66.

Rangarajan, A., Smith, K., Borkum, E., O'Neil, S., and Christensen, A. (2011). Measurement, learning, and evaluation framework for the Bihar Initiative.

*Mathematica Policy Research*. Retrieved from www.mathematica.org/download -media?MediaItemId=%7BD2B5BD53-3666-449F-A27E-48B8ACD5D036%7D

Salamon, L.M. and Newhouse, C.M. (2019) The 2019 Nonprofit Employment Report. Johns Hopkins Center for Civil Society Studies. Retrieved from: https:// philanthropydelaware.org/resources/Documents/The%202019%20Nonprofit %20Employment%20Report%20-%20Nonprofit%20Economic%20Data %20Bulletin%20-%20John%20Hopkins%20Center%20for%20Civil%20Society %20Studies%20_1.8.2019.pdf

Salamon, L. M., & Sokolowski, S. W. (2016). The size and scope of the European third sector. Brussels: European Union FP7 (grant agreement 613034). Third Sector Impact.

Shams-Lau. J., Leu, J., and Le. V. (2018). *Unicorns Unite: How Nonprofits and Foundations Can Build EPIC Partnerships*. Glasgow: Red Press.

Silver, I. (2005). *Unequal Partnerships: Beyond the Rhetoric of Philanthropic Collaboration*. Abingdon: Routledge.

Social Innovation Partnership (2017). Moving On Up: Evaluation report. Retrieved from https://trustforlondon.fra1.digitaloceanspaces.com/media/documents/FinalMoving -on-Up-evaluation-report-Final.pdf

Spencer-Hwang, R., Soret, S., Valladares, J., Torres, X., Pasco-Rubio, M., Dougherty, M., Kim, W., and Montgomery, S. (2016). Strategic partnerships for change in an environmental justice community: The ENRRICH study. *Progress in Community Health Partnerships*, *10*(4), 541–550.

Statista Research Department (2021). Nonprofit organizations in the U.S.: Statistics and facts. Retrieved from www.statista.com/topics/1390/nonprofit-organizations-in -the-us/

Steckel, R. and Simons, R. (1992). *Doing Best by Doing Good: How to Use Public Purpose Partnerships to Boost Corporate Profits and Benefit Your Community*. New York: E.P. Dutton.

Thornberg, C., Kleinheinz, R., Meux, E., and Paik, C. (2017). Central 710 FWY Corridor: An asset based analysis. Beacon Economics. Retrieved from https:// development.patbrowninstitute.org/wp-content/uploads/2017/02/710-Corridor -FWY-Report.pdf

United Nations Foundations, Human Reproduction Programme, and VillageReach (2016). Chipatala Cha Pa Foni Healthcare Through Mobile Phones. Retrieved from www.villagereach.org/wp-content/uploads/2016/08/CCPF-Case-Study-UN -Foundation.pdf

Urban Institute (2020) The Nonprofit Sector in Brief 2019. Retrieved from: https://nccs .urban.org/publication/nonprofit-sector-brief-2019#the-nonprofit-sector-in-brief -2019

Van Tulder, R. and Keen, N. (2018). Capturing collaborative challenges: Designing complexity-sensitive theories of change for cross-sector partnerships. *Journal of Business Ethics*, *150*(2), 315–332.

Van Tulder, R., Seitanidi, M., Crane, A., and Brammer, S. (2016). Enhancing the impact of cross-sector partnerships: Four impact loops for channeling partnership studies. *Journal of Business Ethics*, *135*(1), 1–17.

Warner, M. and Sullivan, R. (eds) (2017). *Putting Partnerships to Work: Strategic Alliances for Development between Government, the Private Sector and Civil Society*. London: Routledge.

# Index

Printed and bound by CPI Group (UK) Ltd, Croydon, CR0 4YY

16/04/2025

14658432-0004